JUMP Math 4.2

Book 4 Part 2 of 2

Contents

jump math

MULTIPLYING POTENTIAL.

A note to educators, parents, and everyone who believes that numeracy is as important as literacy for a fully functioning society

Welcome to JUMP Math

Entering the world of JUMP Math means believing that every child has the capacity to be fully numerate and to love math. Founder and mathematician John Mighton has used this premise to develop his innovative teaching method. The resulting resources isolate and describe concepts so clearly and incrementally that everyone can understand them.

JUMP Math is comprised of teacher's guides (which are the heart of our program), interactive whiteboard lessons, student assessment & practice books, evaluation materials, outreach programs, and teacher training. The Common Core Editions of our resources have been carefully designed to cover the Common Core State Standards. All of this is presented on the JUMP Math web site: **www.jumpmath.org**.

Teacher's guides are available on the web site for free use. Read the introduction to the teacher's guides before you begin using these resources. This will ensure that you understand both the philosophy and the methodology of JUMP Math. The assessment & practice books are designed for use by students, with adult guidance. Each student will have unique needs and it is important to provide the student with the appropriate support and encouragement as he or she works through the material.

Allow students to discover the concepts by themselves as much as possible. Mathematical discoveries can be made in small, incremental steps. The discovery of a new step is like untangling the parts of a puzzle. It is exciting and rewarding.

Children will need to answer the questions marked with a ▯ in a notebook. Grid paper notebooks should always be on hand for answering extra questions or when additional room for calculation is needed.

Contents

Unit 3: Operations and Algebraic Thinking

Unit 4: Number and Operations in Base Ten

Unit 5: Operations and Algebraic Thinking

Unit 6: Measurement and Data

Unit 7: Geometry

PART 2
Unit 1: Operations and Algebraic Thinking

Unit 2: Number and Operations in Base Ten

Unit 3: Operations and Algebraic Thinking

Unit 4: Number and Operations—Fractions

Unit 5: Measurement and Data

Unit 6: Operations and Algebraic Thinking

Unit 7: Number and Operations—Fractions

Unit 8: Measurement and Data

Unit 9: Geometry

OA4-26 Patterns in the Times Tables

The multiples of 8 are 0, 8, 16, 24, ….

1. a) Write the multiples of 8 from 8 to 40 in the first column. Write the next five multiples of 8 in the second column.

   _0_ _8_   ___ ___
   _1_ _6_   ___ ___
   ___ ___   ___ ___
   ___ ___   ___ ___
   ___ ___   ___ ___

   b) What pattern do you see in the ones digits of each column?

   _____

   REMINDER ▶ To find the number of tens, cover the ones digit.

   Example: The number of tens in 168 is 16.

   c) What pattern do you see in the number of tens?

   _____

   d) Use the patterns you found in parts b) and c) to write the multiples of 8 from 88 to 160.

   ___ ___   ___ ___
   ___ ___   ___ ___
   ___ ___   ___ ___
   ___ ___   ___ ___
   ___ ___   ___ ___

2. Are all multiples of 8 even? Explain.

3. Finn calculated $7 \times 8 = 55$ by skip counting. How can you tell right away that he has made a mistake?

BONUS ▶

   a) Write down the first five multiples of 16. Are they also multiples of 8?

   b) Are all multiples of 16 even? Explain.

The multiples of 12 are the numbers you say when you count by 12s: 0, 12, 24, 36, ….

4. a) Write the first five multiples of 12 in the first column of the table. Write the next ten multiples of 12 in the second and third columns.

_0_ _0_	_6_ _0_	___ ___ ___
_1_ _2_	___ ___	___ ___ ___
___ ___	___ ___	___ ___ ___
___ ___	___ ___	___ ___ ___
___ ___	___ ___ ___	___ ___ ___

b) What pattern do you see in the ones digits in each column?

_____

REMINDER ▶ To find the number of tens, cover the ones digit.
Example: The number of tens in 168 is 16.

c) What pattern do you see in the number of tens in each column?

_____

d) What pattern do you see in the first row of the table?

The numbers in the first row are multiples of _____.

e) Use the patterns you found to write the next ten multiples of 12.

_1_ _8_ _0_   ___ ___ ___
___ ___ ___   ___ ___ ___
___ ___ ___   ___ ___ ___
___ ___ ___   ___ ___ ___
___ ___ ___   ___ ___ ___

f) Are all multiples of 12 even? Explain.

_____

_____

BONUS ▶ Add the digits in each multiple of 12 on this page. The answers are all multiples of the same number. What number is that? _____

OA4-27 Advanced Patterns

To extend a pattern, first find the gaps between the terms.

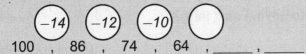

100 , 86 , 74 , 64 , _____ , _____

Each gap is 2 less than the gap before it.
The next two gaps are $10 - 2 = 8$ and $8 - 2 = 6$.

Now extend the pattern itself: 100 , 86 , 74 , 64 , _56_ , _50_ .

1. Write the gaps between the numbers in the sequence. Extend the pattern in the
   gaps. Then extend the sequence itself.

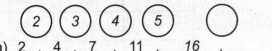

a) 2 , 4 , 7 , 11 , _16_ , _____

b) 3 , 4 , 6 , 9 , 13 , _____ , _____

c) 11 , 14 , 19 , 26 , _____ , _____

d) 6 , 8 , 12 , 18 , 26 , _____ , _____

e) 17 , 16 , 14 , 11 , _____ , _____

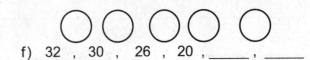

f) 32 , 30 , 26 , 20 , _____ , _____

BONUS ▶

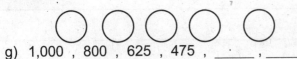

g) 1,000 , 800 , 625 , 475 , _____ , _____

h) 1 , 1 , 2 , 3 , 5 , 8 , _____ , _____

2. a) Complete the T-table for figures 3 and 4. Write the number
      of squares added each time in the circles to the right of the table.

   b) Use the pattern in the gaps to predict the number of shaded
      squares in figures 5 and 6.

Figure	Number of Squares
1	1
2	4
3	
4	
5	
6	

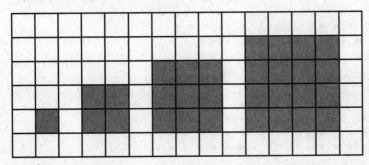

Figure 1   Figure 2   Figure 3   Figure 4

3. Ahmed made a pattern starting at 2 by multiplying.

2 , 4 , 8 , 16 , _____ , _____ , _____ , _____

   a) What number did Ahmed multiply each term by to get the next term? _____

   b) Continue Ahmed's pattern.

   c) Find the gap between the terms. What do you notice? _____

4. Olivia and Krishna save the amounts shown in the chart.

   a) What is the pattern rule for the amount Krishna saves?

   _____

   b) What is the pattern rule for the amount Olivia saves?

   _____

   c) Who do you think will have saved more by the end
   of the seven weeks?

   _____

   d) Continue the patterns in the chart. Were you right?

   _____

Week	Olivia	Krishna
1	$1	$15
2	$2	$20
3	$4	$25
4	$8	$30
5		
6		
7		

5. Look at this pattern: 3 , 6 , 4 , 7 , 5 , 8 , _____ , _____ , _____

   a) Describe how the gap changes in the pattern. _____

   _____

   b) Fill in the blanks to continue the pattern.

6. Make a T-table to predict how many dots will be needed for the 7th figure.

   a) Figure 1   Figure 2   Figure 3   Figure 4

   b) Figure 1   Figure 2   Figure 3   Figure 4

7. Jane runs for 10 minutes on Monday. Each day she runs for 2 minutes longer.
   How many minutes in all did she run in the first four days of the week?

Operations and Algebraic Thinking 4-27

NBT4-40 Remainders

Ori wants to share 7 strawberries with 2 friends.
He sets out 3 plates, one for himself and one for each of his friends.
He puts one strawberry at a time on each plate:

  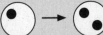   **There is one strawberry left over.**

7 strawberries cannot be divided equally into 3 sets. Each friend gets 2 strawberries, but one is left over.

$$7 \div 3 = 2 \text{ Remainder } 1$$

1. Can 2 people share 5 strawberries equally? Show your work using dots and circles.

2. Share the dots as equally as possible among the circles.
   Note: In one question, the dots can be shared equally (so there's no remainder).

   a) 7 dots in 2 circles

   _____ dots in each circle; _____ dot remaining

   b) 10 dots in 3 circles

   _____ dots in each circle; _____ dot remaining

   c) 10 dots in 5 circles

   _____ dots in each circle; _____ dots remaining

   d) 9 dots in 4 circles

   _____ dots in each circle; _____ dot remaining

   e) 12 dots in 5 circles

   _____ dots in each circle; _____ dots remaining

   f) 13 dots in 4 circles

   _____ dots in each circle; _____ dot remaining

3. Share the dots as equally as possible. Draw a picture and write a division equation.

a) 7 dots in 3 circles

b) 11 dots in 3 circles

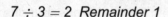

$7 \div 3 = 2$ *Remainder 1*

c) 14 dots in 3 circles

d) 10 dots in 6 circles

e) 10 dots in 4 circles

f) 13 dots in 5 circles

4. Three friends want to share 7 cherries. How many cherries will each friend receive? How many will be left over? Show your work and write a division equation.

5. Find two different ways to share 13 granola bars into equal groups so that one is left over.

6. Fred, George, and Paul have fewer than 10 oranges and more than 3 oranges. They share the oranges equally. How many oranges do they have? Is there more than one answer?

Number and Operations in Base Ten 4-40

NBT4-41 Finding Remainders on Number Lines

Paul has 14 oranges. He wants to sell them in bags of 4. He skip counts to find out how many bags he can sell.

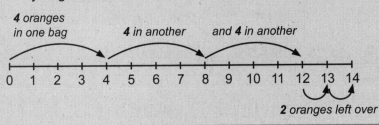

4 oranges in one bag   *4 in another*   and *4 in another*

2 oranges left over

14 oranges divided into sets of size 4 gives 3 sets (with 2 oranges **remaining**)

14 ÷ 4 = 3 Remainder 2

Size of skip   *Number of skips*

1. Fill in the missing numbers.

a)
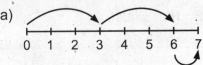

Size of skip = _____

Number of skips = _____

Remainder = _____

b)
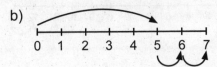

Size of skip = _____

Number of skips = _____

Remainder = _____

c)
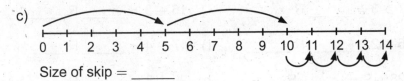

Size of skip = _____

Number of skips = _____

Remainder = _____

2. Write the division equation.

a)
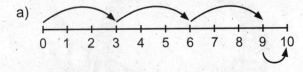

_____

b)
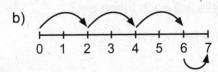

_____

3. Jane has 11 oranges. She wants to make bags of 4.

How many bags can she make? _____

How many oranges will be left over? _____

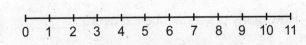

4. On grid paper, draw a number line picture to show the division.

   a) 5 ÷ 2 = 2 Remainder 1   b) 9 ÷ 4 = 2 Remainder 1   c) 11 ÷ 3 = 3 Remainder 2

Number and Operations in Base Ten 4-41

Nina wants to find $13 \div 5$ mentally.

Step 1: Nina counts by 5s. She stops when counting more would pass 13.

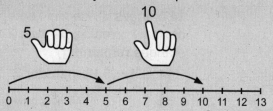

She has two fingers up.

$13 \div 5 = \underline{\ \ 2\ \ }$ Remainder $\underline{\ \ \ \ }$

Step 2: Nina stops counting at 10. She subtracts 10 from 13 to find the remainder.

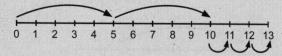

$13 \div 5 = \underline{\ \ 2\ \ }$ Remainder $\underline{\ \ 3\ \ }$

5. Divide by skip counting.

   a) $18 \div 5 = \underline{\ \ \ \ \ }$ R $\underline{\ \ \ \ \ }$

   b) $23 \div 5 = \underline{\ \ \ \ \ }$ R $\underline{\ \ \ \ \ }$

   c) $26 \div 5 = \underline{\ \ \ \ \ }$ R $\underline{\ \ \ \ \ }$

   d) $28 \div 5 = \underline{\ \ \ \ \ }$ R $\underline{\ \ \ \ \ }$

   e) $16 \div 5 = \underline{\ \ \ \ \ }$ R $\underline{\ \ \ \ \ }$

   f) $6 \div 5 = \underline{\ \ \ \ \ }$ R $\underline{\ \ \ \ \ }$

   g) $10 \div 3 = \underline{\ \ \ \ \ }$ R $\underline{\ \ \ \ \ }$

   h) $7 \div 3 = \underline{\ \ \ \ \ }$ R $\underline{\ \ \ \ \ }$

   i) $16 \div 3 = \underline{\ \ \ \ \ }$ R $\underline{\ \ \ \ \ }$

   j) $8 \div 2 = \underline{\ \ \ \ \ }$ R $\underline{\ \ \ \ \ }$

   k) $5 \div 2 = \underline{\ \ \ \ \ }$ R $\underline{\ \ \ \ \ }$

   l) $17 \div 4 = \underline{\ \ \ \ \ }$ R $\underline{\ \ \ \ \ }$

   m) $16 \div 7 = \underline{\ \ \ \ \ }$ R $\underline{\ \ \ \ \ }$

   n) $28 \div 9 = \underline{\ \ \ \ \ }$ R $\underline{\ \ \ \ \ }$

   o) $25 \div 8 = \underline{\ \ \ \ \ }$ R $\underline{\ \ \ \ \ }$

   p) $13 \div 2 = \underline{\ \ \ \ \ }$ R $\underline{\ \ \ \ \ }$

   q) $45 \div 8 = \underline{\ \ \ \ \ }$ R $\underline{\ \ \ \ \ }$

   r) $63 \div 7 = \underline{\ \ \ \ \ }$ R $\underline{\ \ \ \ \ }$

6. Richard wants to divide 16 pencils among 5 friends.

   How many pencils will each friend get? $\underline{\ \ \ \ \ \ \ \ }$

   How many will be left over? $\underline{\ \ \ \ \ \ \ \ }$

7. You have 17 tickets for rides at an amusement park. Each ride takes 5 tickets.

   How many rides can you go on? $\underline{\ \ \ \ \ \ \ \ }$

   How many tickets will be left over? $\underline{\ \ \ \ \ \ \ \ }$

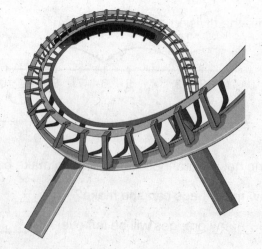

REMINDER ▶ To divide by 3, make groups of 3. Stop when no more groups of 3 can be made.

---

1. Can one more group of 3 be made? If yes, correct the division equation.

a) $7 \div 3 = 1 \, R \, 4$

___yes___ so $7 \div 3 = $ ___2___ R ___1___

b) $11 \div 3 = 2 \, R \, 5$

_____ so $11 \div 3 = $ _____ R _____

c) $13 \div 3 = 4 \, R \, 1$

_____ so $13 \div 3 = $ _____ R _____

d) $9 \div 3 = 2 \, R \, 3$

_____ so $9 \div 3 = $ _____ R _____

2. Can one more group of 4 be made? If yes, correct the division equation.

$16 \div 4 = 3 \, R \, 4$

_____ so $16 \div 4 = $ _____ R _____

3. Make sure the remainder is less than the number being divided by.
Correct the answers that are wrong.

a) $17 \div 5 = 2 \, R \, 7$

$17 \div 5 = $ _____ R _____

b) $24 \div 5 = 3 \, R \, 9$

$24 \div 5 = $ _____ R _____

c) $30 \div 6 = 4 \, R \, 6$

$30 \div 6 = $ _____ R _____

BONUS ▶ $42 \div 5 = 6 \, R \, 12$

$42 \div 5 = $ _____ R _____

Remember: You can write multiplication and division equations from this picture:

$2 \times 4 = 8$

$8 \div 4 = 2$

You can also write equations from pictures with leftover dots:

$(2 \times 4) + 1 = 9$

$9 \div 4 = 2 \, R \, 1$

---

4. Write two equations for each picture.

a)

_____

_____

b)

_____

_____

c)

_____

_____

---

5. Draw a picture for the division equation. Then write an equation with multiplication and addition.

   a) 13 ÷ 5 = 2 R 3

   b) 17 ÷ 5 = 3 R 2

   c) 19 ÷ 4 = 4 R 3

   _(2 × 5) + 3 = 13_   _____   _____

6. Fill in the blanks. Then write an equation with multiplication and addition.

   a) 19 ÷ 5 = 3 R 4

   __5__ in each group

   __3__ groups

   __4__ left over

   __19__ total

   _(5 × 3) + 4 = 19_

   b) 11 ÷ 4 = 2 R 3

   _____ in each group

   _____ groups

   _____ left over

   _____ total

   _____

   c) 21 ÷ 4 = 5 R 1

   _____ in each group

   _____ groups

   _____ left over

   _____ total

   _____

7. a) Mia wants to find the total number of objects in groups. Circle the numbers she should multiply together.

   i) 19 ÷ ③ = ⑥ R 1   ii) 16 ÷ 5 = 3 R 1   iii) 23 ÷ 5 = 4 R 3

   b) Write an equation with multiplication and addition for each division equation in part a).

   i) _(3 × 6) + 1 = 19_   ii) _____   iii) _____

8. Divide. Check your answer.

   a) 10 ÷ 3   b) 12 ÷ 5   c) 17 ÷ 5   d) 21 ÷ 8   e) 18 ÷ 5   f) 20 ÷ 5

   g) 52 ÷ 8   h) 38 ÷ 6   i) 73 ÷ 8   j) 54 ÷ 7   k) 56 ÷ 9   l) 64 ÷ 7

   BONUS ▶ 130 ÷ 12

9. Nine people share 60 pennies. How many does each person get? How many are left over?

10. Sohrab writes 35 ÷ 5 = 6 R 5. What's wrong with Sohrab's equation? How would you rewrite it?

NBT4-43 Dividing Using Tens, Hundreds, and Thousands

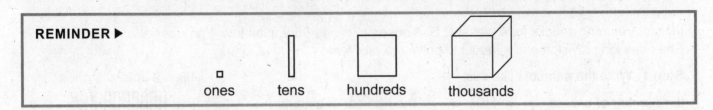

REMINDER ▶

ones tens hundreds thousands

1. Divide the blocks among 2 equal groups. Then write the division equation.

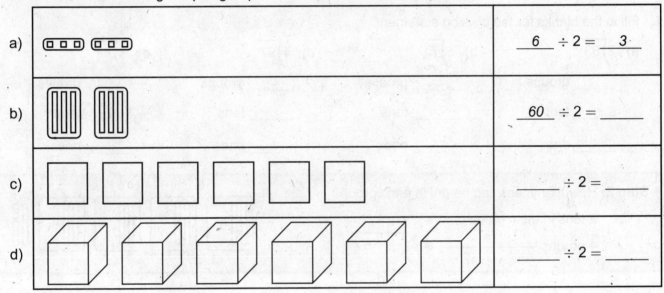

a) $\underline{6} \div 2 = \underline{3}$

b) $\underline{60} \div 2 = \underline{}$

c) $\underline{} \div 2 = \underline{}$

d) $\underline{} \div 2 = \underline{}$

2. a) Divide 8 tens among 4 equal groups. Then finish the division equation.

   8 tens ÷ 4 = $\underline{2}$ tens   so 80 ÷ 4 = $\underline{20}$

   b) Divide 12 hundreds among 3 equal groups. Then finish the division equation.

   12 hundreds ÷ 3 = $\underline{}$ hundreds   so 1,200 ÷ 3 = $\underline{}$

   c) Divide 8 thousands among 2 equal groups. Then finish the division equation.

   8 thousands ÷ 2 = $\underline{}$ thousands   so $\underline{}$ ÷ 2 = $\underline{}$

3. Divide.

   a) 9 ÷ 3 = $\underline{}$

   90 ÷ 3 = $\underline{}$

   900 ÷ 3 = $\underline{}$

   9,000 ÷ 3 = $\underline{}$

   b) 20 ÷ 4 = $\underline{}$

   200 ÷ 4 = $\underline{}$

   2,000 ÷ 4 = $\underline{}$

   20,000 ÷ 4 = $\underline{}$

   BONUS ▶ 560,000,000 ÷ 8 = $\underline{}$

Inez is preparing snacks for 4 classes. She needs to divide 95 apples into 4 groups. She uses long division and a model to solve the problem.

Step 1: Write the numbers like this:

the number of groups ⟶ 4)95 ⟵ the number of objects to divide into groups

$95 = 9$ tens $+ 5$ ones

1. Fill in the blanks for the division statement.

   a) 2)53

   _____ groups

   _____ tens

   _____ ones

   b) 5)71

   _____ groups

   _____ tens

   _____ ones

   c) 4)97

   _____ groups

   _____ tens

   _____ ones

   d) 5)88

   _____ groups

   _____ tens

   _____ ones

Step 2: How many tens can be put in each group?

2 tens in each group ⟶

4 groups ⟶

	2	
4)	9	5

2. For each division problem, write how many groups have been made and how many tens are in each group.

   a)

   4)5 5

   _____ groups

   _____ ten in each group

   b)

   5)9 7

   _____ groups

   _____ ten in each group

   c)

   3)7 6

   _____ groups

   _____ tens in each group

   d)

   3)8 9

   _____ groups

   _____ tens in each group

3. How many tens can be put in each group?

   a)

   | | 2 | |
   | 4) | 8 | 7 |

   b)

   3)9 4

   c)

   6)7 4

   d)

   2)9 8

   e)

   2)8 5

   f)

   3)6 7

   g)

   8)9 1

   h)
   3)8 2

Step 3: How many tens have been placed into groups altogether?

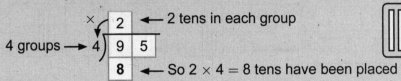

2 × 4 = 8

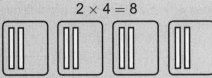

× ↗ 2 ← 2 tens in each group

4 groups → 4⟌9 5

8 ← So 2 × 4 = 8 tens have been placed

4. Multiply to decide how many tens have been placed.

a)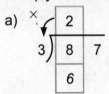

b)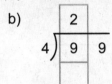

c)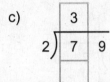

d)
2⟌8 9 with 4 on top

5. Multiply to decide how many tens have been placed. Then answer the questions.

a)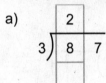

How many groups? _____

How many tens? _____

How many tens in each group? _____

How many tens placed altogether? _____

b)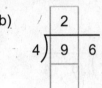

How many groups? _____

How many tens? _____

How many tens in each group? _____

How many tens placed altogether? _____

6. Skip count to find out how many tens can be placed in each group. Then multiply to find out how many tens have been placed.

a)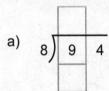

b)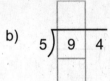

c)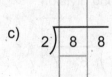

d) 7⟌9 5

e) 4⟌8 5

f)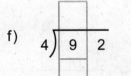

g) 5⟌6 3

h) 2⟌9 8

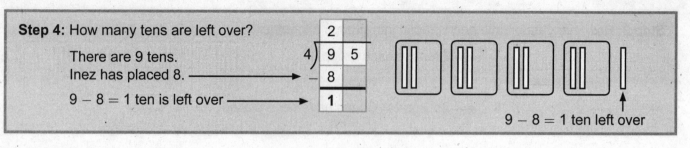

Step 4: How many tens are left over?

There are 9 tens.

Inez has placed 8. ——————————————➤

9 − 8 = 1 ten is left over ——————————➤

$$4\overline{)\,9\;5\;}$$ 2, − 8, **1**

9 − 8 = 1 ten left over

---

7. Carry out the first four steps of long division.

a)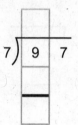
$$7\overline{)\,9\;7\,}$$

b)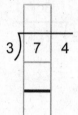
$$3\overline{)\,7\;4\,}$$

c)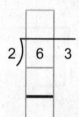
$$2\overline{)\,6\;3\,}$$

d)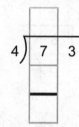
$$4\overline{)\,7\;3\,}$$

e)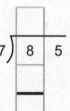
$$7\overline{)\,8\;5\,}$$

f)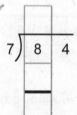
$$7\overline{)\,8\;4\,}$$

g)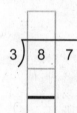
$$3\overline{)\,8\;7\,}$$

h)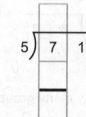
$$5\overline{)\,7\;1\,}$$

Step 5: There are 1 ten and 5 ones left over.
So there are 15 ones left over.

Write 5 beside the 1 to show this.

$$4\overline{)\,9\;5\,}$$ 2, − 8↓, **1 5**

There are 15 ones still to place

---

8. Carry out the first five steps of long division.

a)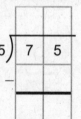
$$5\overline{)\,7\;5\,}$$

b)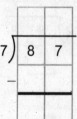
$$7\overline{)\,8\;7\,}$$

c)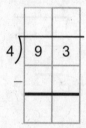
$$4\overline{)\,9\;3\,}$$

d)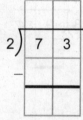
$$2\overline{)\,7\;3\,}$$

e)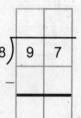
$$8\overline{)\,9\;7\,}$$

f)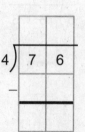
$$4\overline{)\,7\;6\,}$$

g)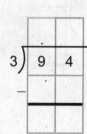
$$3\overline{)\,9\;4\,}$$

h)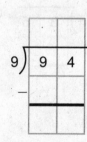
$$9\overline{)\,9\;4\,}$$

Step 6: How many of the 15 ones can be placed in each group?

Divide to find out.

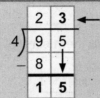

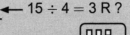 15 ÷ 4 = 3 R ?

How many ones are left over? ⟶ ?

9. Carry out the first six steps of long division.

a)
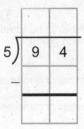

b)
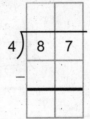

c)
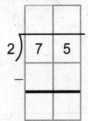

d)
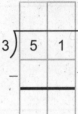

e)
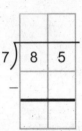

f)
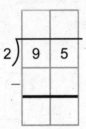

g)
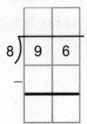

h)
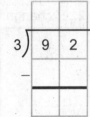

Step 7: How many ones are left over?

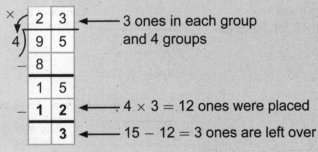

3 ones in each group and 4 groups

4 × 3 = 12 ones were placed

15 − 12 = 3 ones are left over

95 ÷ 4 = 23 with 3 left over

left over ⟶

10. Carry out all seven steps of long division.

a)
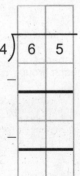

b)
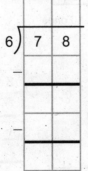

c)
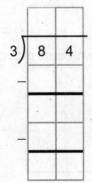

d)

11. a) How many weeks are there in 84 days?

b) A boat can hold 4 children. How many boats will 72 children need?

NBT4-45 Long Division—Multi-Digit by 1-Digit

When drawing pictures in math, you need to make them simple.

Example: A picture of 335 shown with hundreds blocks, tens blocks, and ones blocks:

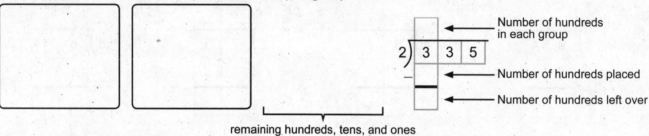

1. Find 335 ÷ 2 by using a base ten model.

Step 1: Divide the hundreds squares into 2 equal groups.

remaining hundreds, tens, and ones

Number of hundreds in each group

Number of hundreds placed

Number of hundreds left over

Step 2: Exchange the leftover hundreds square for 10 tens.

exchange a hundred for 10 tens

Number of tens to be placed

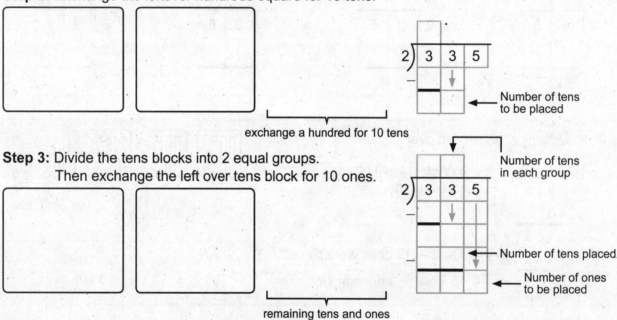

Step 3: Divide the tens blocks into 2 equal groups.
Then exchange the left over tens block for 10 ones.

remaining tens and ones

exchange a ten for 10 ones

Number of tens in each group

Number of tens placed

Number of ones to be placed

Step 4: Divide the ones into two equal groups.

remaining ones

Number of ones in each group

Number of ones placed

Number of ones left over

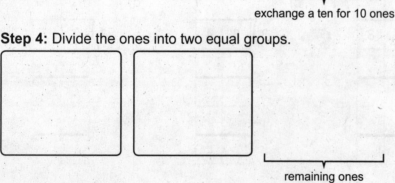

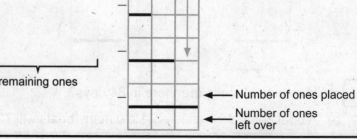

So 335 ÷ 2 = _____ R _____

2. Divide.

a)

b)
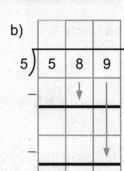

c)

d)
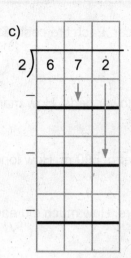

3. Divide. There will be fewer hundreds than the number of groups. Write "0" in the hundreds position to show this. The first one has been started for you.

a)
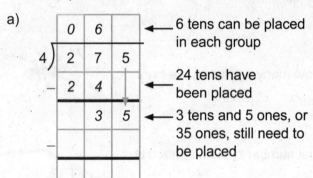
6 tens can be placed in each group

24 tens have been placed

3 tens and 5 ones, or 35 ones, still need to be placed

b)
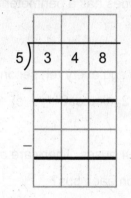

c)
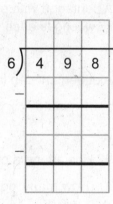

d)
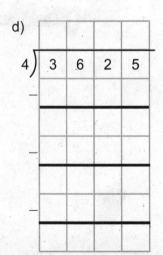

e)
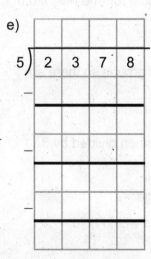

f)
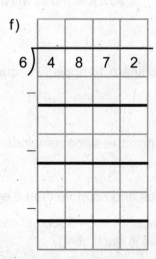

g)
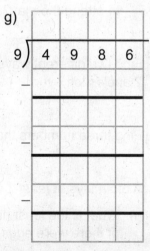

4. Divide using long division.

a) $8,421 \div 3$

b) $3,462 \div 5$

c) $6,103 \div 4$

d) $21,047 \div 3$

5. A boat can hold 6 children. How many boats will 372 children need?

NBT4-46 Concepts in Multiplication and Division

1. Tom needs new tires for his car. Each tire costs $263. How much do all 4 tires cost?

2. Jennifer plants 84 lilies in 4 flower beds. How many lilies are in each flower bed?

3. A square park has a perimeter of 680 m. How long is each side of the park?

4. Jerry paid $276 for 6 sweaters. How much did each sweater cost?

5. Each side of a square field is 874 m long. What is the perimeter of the field?

6. A pentagon with equal sides has a perimeter of 325 cm. How long is each side?

7. A queen ant can lay one egg every ten seconds. How many eggs can she lay in …

   a) 1 minute?   b) 2 minutes?   c) an hour?

8. 92 kids attend a play on 4 buses. There are an equal number of kids on each bus.

   a) How many kids are on each bus?

   b) A ticket for the play costs $6. How much will it cost for one busload of kids to attend the play?

9. Find two different ways to share 14 apples in equal groups so there are 2 apples left over.

10. Find three numbers that give the same remainder when divided by 3.

11. A robin lays at *least* 3 eggs and *no more* than 6 eggs.

   a) What is the least number of eggs 3 robins' nests would hold (if there were eggs laid in each nest)?

   b) What is the greatest number of eggs 3 robins' nests would hold?

   c) Three robins' nests contain 13 eggs. Draw a picture to show 2 ways the eggs could be shared among the nests.

NBT4-47 Mental Math

1. Find the missing number in the multiplication. Then divide.

   a) 300 × _____ = 3,000

      so 3,000 ÷ 300 = _____

   b) 40 × _____ = 4,000

      so 4,000 ÷ 40 = _____

   c) 20 × _____ = 20,000

      so 20,000 ÷ 20 = _____

   d) 600 × _____ = 60,000

      so 60,000 ÷ 600 = _____

2. Divide mentally.

   a) 9,000 ÷ 900

      = _____

   b) 6,000 ÷ 60

      = _____

   c) 80,000 ÷ 80

      = _____

   d) 70,000 ÷ 700

      = _____

   BONUS ▶ 80,000,000 ÷ 800 = _____

To find 86 ÷ 2, divide the tens and ones separately.

86 ÷ 2	=	80 ÷ 2	+	6 ÷ 2
43	=	40	+	3

---

3. Divide one place value at a time.

   a) 64 ÷ 2 = (60 ÷ 2) + (4 ÷ 2)

      = _30_ + _2_

      = _32_

   b) 69 ÷ 3 = (60 ÷ 3) + (9 ÷ 3)

      = _____ + _____

      = _____

   c) 86 ÷ 2 = (80 ÷ 2) + (6 ÷ 2)

      = _____ + _____

      = _____

   d) 96 ÷ 3 = (_____ ÷ 3) + (_____ ÷ 3)

      = _____ + _____

      = _____

   BONUS ▶ 824 ÷ 2 = (800 ÷ 2) + (20 ÷ 2) + (4 ÷ 2)

4. Check your answer to Question 3 a) and b) by multiplication.

   a)
      ◀— Is this 64? ✓ _____

   b)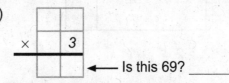
      ◀— Is this 69? _____

NBT4-48 Mental Math (Advanced)

A rectangle with 4 squares down and
6 squares across has 24 squares in total.

$4 \times 6 = 24$ so $24 \div 4 = 6$

1. How many squares across is the rectangle?

a)

$12 \div 3 =$ _____

b)

$15 \div 3 =$ _____

2. Draw the rectangle to make the total number of squares. How many
squares across do you need?

a)

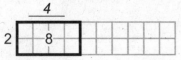

b)

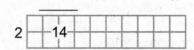

3. Decide how many squares across you need to make the rectangle. Then write
the division equation.

a)   5
4 | 20 |

$20 \div 4 = 5$

b)
4 | 200 |

_____

c)
4 | 2,000 |

_____

d)
4 | 20,000 |

_____

Tara finds $36 \div 2$ by splitting 36 into tens and ones.

$36 = 30 + 6$ so
$36 \div 2 = 15 + 3 = 18$

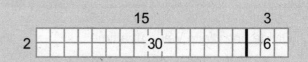

4. Use Tara's method to divide.

a) $92 \div 2$

    _45_ + _1_
2 | 90 | 2 |

$92 \div 2 =$ _46_

b) $56 \div 2$

    _____ + _____
2 | 50 | 6 |

$56 \div 2 =$ _____

c) $62 \div 2$

    _____ + _____

$62 \div 2 =$ _____

d) $74 \div 2$

    _____ + _____

$74 \div 2 =$ _____

Ron uses Tara's method to divide 78 ÷ 2, but...

... he chooses the tens and ones so that the **number of tens** is a multiple of the **number that he is dividing by**.

He uses the largest number of tens he can.

78 = 7 tens + 8 ones

 = **6** tens + 18 ones

  ↖ **6** is a multiple of **2**

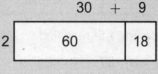

So 78 ÷ 2 = 39

5. Use Ron's method to divide.

a) 94 ÷ 2

 94 = 9 tens + 4 ones

  = 8 tens + _____ ones

  ↑

 8 is a multiple of 2

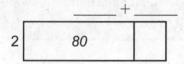

94 ÷ 2 = _____

b) 84 ÷ 3

 84 = 8 tens + 4 ones

  = 6 tens + _____ ones

  ↑

 6 is a multiple of 3

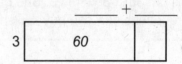

84 ÷ 3 = _____

c) 58 ÷ 2

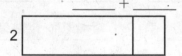

58 ÷ 2 = _____

d) 51 ÷ 3

51 ÷ 3 = _____

e) 72 ÷ 3

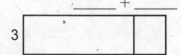

72 ÷ 3 = _____

f) 96 ÷ 4

96 ÷ 4 = _____

6. A rectangular patio floor is covered with 84 tiles in 6 rows.
How many tiles are in each row?

So there are _____ tiles in each row.

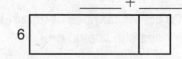

NBT4-49 Interpreting Remainders

dividend   divisor   quotient   remainder

$$35 \div 8 = 4 \text{ R } 3$$

1. Circle the quotient. Underline the remainder.

   a) $42 \div 8 = 5 \text{ R } 2$ b) $27 \div 4 = 6 \text{ R } 3$ c) $31 \div 9 = 3 \text{ R } 4$ d) $15 \div 2 = 7 \text{ R } 1$

Sometimes the answer to a division problem is the quotient without the remainder.
Example: Jiba has $35. How many $8 T-shirts can she buy?

Solution: Skip count until the T-shirts cost too much money.

    $8 $16 $24 $32 $40 ⟵ This is too much money.

Then write the division: $35 \div 8 = 4 \text{ R } 3$. She can't buy part of a fifth T-shirt, so ignore the remainder.
The answer is the quotient: she can buy 4 T-shirts.

2. Jordan has $28. How many $5 movie tickets can he buy?

   a) Skip count by $5 until the movie tickets cost too much money.

    MOVIE TICKET ADMIT ONE   MOVIE TICKET ADMIT ONE   MOVIE TICKET ADMIT ONE   MOVIE TICKET ADMIT ONE

     $5 $10 $15   _____   _____   _____   _____

   b) $28 \div 5 =$ _____ R _____

   c) How many tickets can Jordan buy? _____

      What part of the division equation is your answer? _____

3. Write a division statement. Then answer the question.

   a) Ahmed has $50. How many $12 T-shirts can he buy?

      $50 \div 12 =$ _____ R _____ , so he can buy _____ T-shirts.

   b) Nancy has $82. How many $6 books can she buy?

      _____ $\div$ _____ $=$ _____ R _____ , so she can buy _____ books.

4. Nina has 20 tickets for rides at an amusement park. Each ride takes 3 tickets.
How many rides can she go on?

                Number and Operations in Base Ten 4-49

Sometimes the answer to a division problem is one more than the quotient.

Example: Each can holds 3 tennis balls. A tennis instructor needs 25 tennis balls.
How many cans does the instructor need to buy?

Solution: Draw 3 tennis balls in each can, until you have 25 tennis balls.

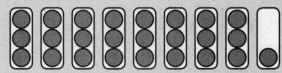

$25 \div 3 = 8$ R 1, so 8 cans are completely filled. You need one more can for the last ball.
So the instructor needs to buy 9 cans altogether.

5. Each can holds 3 tennis balls. A tennis instructor needs 14 tennis balls.

   a) Draw 3 dots in each can until you have 14 dots. Then write the division equation.

   $14 \div 3 = $ _____ R _____

   b) How many cans are completely full? _____

   c) How many cans does the instructor need to buy? _____

6. Ping needs to move 10 boxes. On each trip she can carry 4 boxes.
   How many trips will she need to make?

   _____ ÷ _____ = _____ R _____ , so Ping needs to make _____ trips.

7. Write the division statement. Interpret the remainder to answer the question.

   a) 82 people are going on a bus trip for school. Each bus holds 30 people.
      How many buses are needed?

   b) Ian has $82. Each sweater costs $30. How many sweaters can he buy?

   c) Joni needs to raise $85. She sells pens for $3 each. How many pens does
      she need to sell?

   d) Nomi has 21 kg of salt. She sells it in 2 kg bags. How many bags can she sell?

   e) 10 people are going on a canoe trip. Each canoe can hold 3 people.
      How many canoes do they need?

   f) Siru wants to place her stamps in an album. Each page holds 9 stamps.
      How many pages will she need for 95 stamps?

NBT4-50 Interpreting Remainders (Advanced)

Sometimes the answer to a division problem is the remainder.

Example: Lee has 19 candies. He makes gift bags of 5 each, and he eats the leftover candies. How many candies will he eat?

Solution: $19 \div 5 = 3$ R 4, so Lee makes 3 gift bags and eats 4 candies.

1. Write the division equation and circle the answer to each question.

   a) Juan has 15 apples. He makes gift bags of 4 each and keeps the leftover apples for himself. How many apples did he keep? _____ ÷ _____ = _____ R _____

   b) Serena has 22 apples. She sells as many as she can in baskets of 4. How many apples does she have to sell separately? _____ ÷ _____ = _____ R _____

   c) A store sells broccoli in packs of 4 stalks. They have 59 stalks.

      i) How many packs of broccoli can the store sell? _____ ÷ _____ = _____ R _____

      ii) How many stalks of broccoli do they have to sell separately? _____ ÷ _____ = _____ R _____

2. Write the division equation. Then answer the question.

   a) 26 people are going on a car trip. Each car holds 6 people. $\underline{\quad 26 \div 6 = 4\ R\ 2 \quad}$

      How many cars will they need? __5__

   b) A store has 800 pencils and sells them in packs of 9. _____

      How many packs can they sell? _____

   c) A project requires 25 hours of work. Each volunteer can do 4 hours of work. _____

      How many volunteers are needed? _____

   d) Bilal has $25. Baseballs cost $4. _____

      How many baseballs can he buy? _____

      How much money will he have left over? _____

   e) Esther needs to move 23 boxes. On each trip she can carry 3 boxes. She carries as many as she can each time. _____

      How many trips does she make? _____

      How many boxes does she carry on her last trip? _____

NBT4-51 Extending and Predicting Patterns

1. The **core** of a pattern is the part that repeats. Karen makes the core of several repeating patterns using red blocks (**R**) and yellow blocks (**Y**). Continue her pattern by writing Rs and Ys.

a)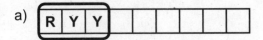

b)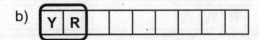

c)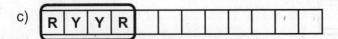

d)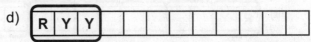

e)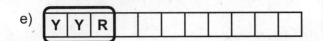

f)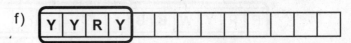

2. Write a division equation to match the picture.

a)

$\underline{\quad 9 \quad} \div \underline{\quad 4 \quad} = \underline{\quad 2 \quad}$ Remainder $\underline{\quad 1 \quad}$

b)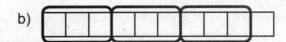

$\underline{\qquad} \div \underline{\qquad} = \underline{\qquad}$ Remainder $\underline{\qquad}$

c)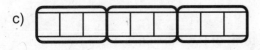

$\underline{\qquad} \div \underline{\qquad} = \underline{\qquad}$ Remainder $\underline{\qquad}$

d)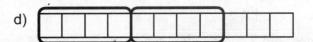

$\underline{\qquad} \div \underline{\qquad} = \underline{\qquad}$ Remainder $\underline{\qquad}$

3. The core is given. Extend the pattern. Circle the core as many times as it occurs. Then write a division equation to match a picture.

a)

$\underline{\quad 10 \quad} \div \underline{\quad 3 \quad} = \underline{\quad 3 \quad}$ Remainder $\underline{\quad 1 \quad}$

b)

$\underline{\qquad} \div \underline{\qquad} = \underline{\qquad}$ Remainder $\underline{\qquad}$

c)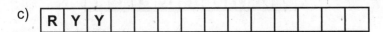

$\underline{\qquad} \div \underline{\qquad} = \underline{\qquad}$ Remainder $\underline{\qquad}$

d)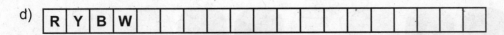

$\underline{\qquad} \div \underline{\qquad} = \underline{\qquad}$ Remainder $\underline{\qquad}$

4. a) Extend each pattern to find the 12th term.

i) | R | W | B | | | | | | | | | | |

ii) | R | R | W | W | | | | | | | | | |

iii) | R | Y | | | | | | | | | | | |

iv) | R | R | Y | W | B | B | | | | | | | |

b) Make a prediction: What is the 12th term of the pattern with core RYWY? _____

Juan predicts the 12th and 14th terms of the pattern with core R R Y W as follows:

| R | R | Y | W | | | | | | | | | | |

$12 \div 4 = 3$ R **0**, so the 12th term is the **last** term of the **3rd** core.

$14 \div 4 = 3$ R **2**

There are **3** cores before the 14th term. The 14th term is the **2nd** term of the next core.

The 12th term is W (white) and the 14th term is R (red).

5. Use division to predict the color of the given block.

a) 19th block

| R | R | Y | Y | Y | R | R | Y | Y | Y |

Color: _____

b) 35th block

| Y | R | Y | Y | R | Y | Y | R | Y |

Color: _____

c) 48th block

| R | R | Y | G | Y | R | R | Y | G | Y |

Color: _____

d) 100th block

| Y | R | W | Y | Y | R | W | Y | Y |

Color: _____

6. a) What is the color of the 41st bead? _____

b) Will the 42nd triangle in this pattern point up or down? _____

Number and Operations in Base Ten 4-51

OA4-28 Introduction to Algebra—Addition

1. Some apples are inside a box and some are outside. Draw the missing apples in the box.

   a)

   total number of apples

   b)

   c)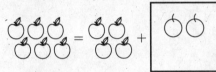

   total number of apples

   d)

2. Draw the missing apples in the box. Then write the missing number in the box.

   a)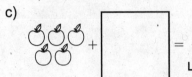

   6   =   4   +   2

   b)

   7   =   3   +   ☐

   c)

   3   +   ☐   =   4

   d)

   4   +   ☐   =   8

Finding the missing number in an equation is called **solving** the equation.

---

3. Draw a picture for the equation. Use your picture to solve the equation.

   a) $5 + \boxed{} = 8$

   b) $\boxed{} + 4 = 10$

4. Solve the equation by guessing and checking.

   a) $\boxed{} + 4 = 7$ b) $3 + \boxed{} = 8$ c) $\boxed{} + 5 = 17$ d) $8 + \boxed{} = 15$

1. Draw the same number of apples in each box. Write the equation for the picture.

a)

$\square + \square = 10$

b)

_____

c)

_____

> Multiplication is a short form for repeated addition. 🍎 + 🍎 + 🍎 is the same as 3 × 🍎
>
> $\boxed{1} + \boxed{1} + \boxed{1}$ is the same as $3 \times \boxed{1}$

2. Draw a picture for the equation. Use your picture to solve the equation.

a)

$3 \times \boxed{4} = 12$

b)

$2 \times \square = 12$

c)

$3 \times \square = 15$

d)

$6 \times \square = 18$

3. How many apples should be in the box? Write the number.

a) $2 \times \boxed{3} = $

b) $2 \times \boxed{} = $

c) $\boxed{} \times 3 = $

d) $\boxed{} \times 4 = $

e) $\boxed{} \times 3 = $

f) $\boxed{} \times 2 = $

g) $3 \times$ $= \boxed{}$ h) $3 \times$ $= \boxed{}$ i) $8 \times$ $= \boxed{}$ j) $7 \times$ $= \boxed{}$

BONUS ▶ There are 10 apples in the bag. What number goes in the box?

$3 \times$ $= \boxed{}$

Use circles instead of apples to make your drawing simpler.

4. Draw a picture of each equation. Then solve the equation using your picture.

a) $3 \times 6 = \boxed{}$

b) $3 \times \boxed{} = 21$

5. Solve the equation by guessing and checking.

a) $5 \times \boxed{} = 30$

b) $\boxed{} \times 2 = 18$

c) $2 \times \boxed{} = 24$

d) $\boxed{} \times 7 = 42$

e) $24 \div \boxed{} = 6$

f) $\boxed{} \div 5 = 6$

g) $5 \times 4 = \boxed{} \times 10$

h) $12 \times 3 = 9 \times \boxed{}$

OA4-30 Totals and Equations

1. Circle the equations where the unknown is by itself.

$x = 7 + 2$ $\qquad$ $w + 5 = 10$ $\qquad$ $5 - 3 = a$ $\qquad$ $6 + b = 4$ $\qquad$ $k = 12 \div 3$

Total or whole			You can write 3 equations for a total and two parts:

Total or whole ⎰ Part 1
⎱ Part 2

You can write 3 equations for a total and two parts:

Total = Part 1 + Part 2

Part 1 = Total − Part 2

Part 2 = Total − Part 1

2. Write three equations for the given information.

a)

	How Many?	Total
Part 1	8	
Part 2	5	w

_____ = _____ + _____
Total   Part 1   Part 2

_____ = _____ − _____
Part 1   Total   Part 2

_____ = _____ − _____
Part 2   Total   Part 1

b)

	How Many?	Total
Part 1	21	
Part 2	w	24

_____ = _____ + _____
Total   Part 1   Part 2

_____ = _____ − _____
Part 1   Total   Part 2

_____ = _____ − _____
Part 2   Total   Part 1

c)

	How Many?	Total
Part 1	w	
Part 2	3	17

_____ = _____ + _____
Total   Part 1   Part 2

_____ = _____ − _____
Part 1   Total   Part 2

_____ = _____ − _____
Part 2   Total   Part 1

d)

	How Many?	Total
Part 1	215	
Part 2	65	w

_____ = _____ + _____
Total   Part 1   Part 2

_____ = _____ − _____
Part 1   Total   Part 2

_____ = _____ − _____
Part 2   Total   Part 1

e)

	How Many?	Total
Part 1	w	
Part 2	18	97

_____ = _____ + _____
Total   Part 1   Part 2

_____ = _____ − _____
Part 1   Total   Part 2

_____ = _____ − _____
Part 2   Total   Part 1

f)

	How Many?	Total
Part 1	78	
Part 2	w	312

_____ = _____ + _____
Total   Part 1   Part 2

_____ = _____ − _____
Part 1   Total   Part 2

_____ = _____ − _____
Part 2   Total   Part 1

3. Circle each equation in Question 2 where the unknown is by itself.

4. Write an equation where w is by itself.

a)

	How Many?	Total
Part 1	12	17
Part 2	w	

_____

b)

	How Many?	Total
Part 1	w	8
Part 2	5	

_____

c)

	How Many?	Total
Part 1	11	w
Part 2	2	

_____

d)

	How Many?	Total
Part 1	w	9
Part 2	3	

_____

5. Fill in the table. Write x for the number you are not given.

		Green Grapes	Purple Grapes	Total Number of Grapes	Equation
a)	7 green grapes 12 grapes in total	7	x	12	$x = 12 - 7$
b)	5 green grapes 3 purple grapes				
c)	11 grapes in total 8 green grapes				
d)	7 purple grapes 13 grapes altogether				
e)	34 purple grapes 21 green grapes				
f)	71 grapes altogether 45 purple grapes				

6. Circle the total in the story. Then write an equation and solve it.

a) 6 green grapes
9 grapes altogether
x purple grapes

$x = 9 - 6$
$x = 3$

b) 3 green grapes
4 purple grapes
x grapes altogether

c) 9 grapes altogether
7 purple grapes
x green grapes

d) There are 6 cats.
There are 12 dogs.
There are x pets altogether.

e) There are 9 marbles.
x of them are red.
5 of them are not red.

f) Sean has 8 cousins.
x of them are boys.
5 cousins are girls.

OA4-31 Differences and Equations

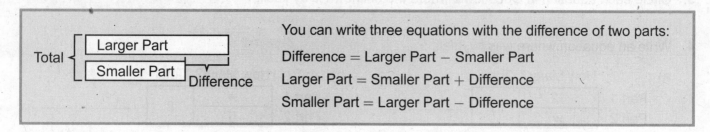

You can write three equations with the difference of two parts:

Difference = Larger Part − Smaller Part
Larger Part = Smaller Part + Difference
Smaller Part = Larger Part − Difference

1. Write three equations for the given information.

a)

	How Many?	Difference
Larger Part	10	
Smaller Part	4	w

$\underline{\hspace{1cm}}_{Difference} = \underline{\hspace{1cm}}_{Larger\ Part} - \underline{\hspace{1cm}}_{Smaller\ Part}$

$\underline{\hspace{1cm}}_{Larger\ Part} = \underline{\hspace{1cm}}_{Smaller\ Part} + \underline{\hspace{1cm}}_{Difference}$

$\underline{\hspace{1cm}}_{Smaller\ Part} = \underline{\hspace{1cm}}_{Larger\ Part} - \underline{\hspace{1cm}}_{Difference}$

b)

	How Many?	Difference
Larger Part	w	
Smaller Part	4	10

$\underline{\hspace{1cm}}_{Difference} = \underline{\hspace{1cm}}_{Larger\ Part} - \underline{\hspace{1cm}}_{Smaller\ Part}$

$\underline{\hspace{1cm}}_{Larger\ Part} = \underline{\hspace{1cm}}_{Smaller\ Part} + \underline{\hspace{1cm}}_{Difference}$

$\underline{\hspace{1cm}}_{Smaller\ Part} = \underline{\hspace{1cm}}_{Larger\ Part} - \underline{\hspace{1cm}}_{Difference}$

c)

	How Many?	Difference
Larger Part	34	
Smaller Part	w	9

$\underline{\hspace{1cm}}_{Difference} = \underline{\hspace{1cm}}_{Larger\ Part} - \underline{\hspace{1cm}}_{Smaller\ Part}$

$\underline{\hspace{1cm}}_{Larger\ Part} = \underline{\hspace{1cm}}_{Smaller\ Part} + \underline{\hspace{1cm}}_{Difference}$

$\underline{\hspace{1cm}}_{Smaller\ Part} = \underline{\hspace{1cm}}_{Larger\ Part} - \underline{\hspace{1cm}}_{Difference}$

2. Circle each equation in Question 1 where the unknown is by itself.

3. Fill in the table. Write x for the number you are not given. Circle the part that is larger.
   Write an equation where the unknown is by itself.

		Parts		Difference	Equation
		Cats	Dogs		
a)	7 cats; 12 more dogs than cats	7	x	12	$x = 12 + 7$
b)	5 cats; 3 dogs				
c)	11 more dogs than cats; 8 cats				
d)	9 dogs; 3 fewer cats than dogs				
e)	17 dogs; 13 fewer dogs than cats				

4. Circle the part that is larger. Write the difference two ways to make an equation.

a) There are (9 hats.)
   There are x scarves.
   There are 4 more hats
   than scarves.

b) There are x hats.
   There are 7 scarves.
   There are 5 fewer hats
   than scarves.

c) There are 5 hats.
   There are 6 scarves.
   There are x fewer hats
   than scarves.

5. Fill in the table. Write x for the number you are not given.

Problem	What Is Compared?	How Many?	Difference	Equation and Solution
a) Sean has 48 American stamps in his collection. He has 12 more American stamps than Canadian stamps. How many Canadian stamps does he have?	American stamps	(48)	12	$x = 48 - 12$ $x = 36$
	Canadian stamps	x		
b) Lina has 12 red marbles. She has 8 green marbles. How many more red marbles than green marbles does she have?				
c) There are 13 dogs in a shelter. There are 7 more cats than dogs in the shelter. How many cats are there?				
d) A bulldog weighs 15 pounds less than a boxer. The boxer weighs 78 pounds. How much does the bulldog weigh?				

6. Write the difference two ways to write an equation. Then solve the equation.

a) Erin hikes 8 miles on Saturday. She hikes 3 miles more on Sunday than on Saturday. How many miles did she hike on Sunday?

b) 17 cars are parked in the school parking lot. There are 8 fewer vans than cars in the same lot. How many vans are there?

c) A dalmatian weighs 65 pounds. A dingo weighs 17 pounds less. How much does the dingo weigh?

d) Cindy biked 42 km on Saturday. On Sunday, she biked 12 km more than on Saturday. How far did she bike on Sunday?

e) Kevin counted 38 robins in his backyard on Monday and 29 robins on Tuesday. How many more robins flew through Kevin's backyard on Monday?

f) Linh counted 72 shooting stars on one night. The next night she saw 24 fewer stars than on the first night. How many shooting stars did she see on the second night?

OA4-32 Addition and Subtraction Word Problems

1. Fill in the table. Write *x* for the number you need to find. Cross out the cell you do not use.

	Problem	Parts	How Many?	Difference / Total	Equation and Solution
a)	Sean has 4 pounds of apples and 5 pounds of pears. How many pounds of fruit does he have?	apples	4 pounds	~~Difference:~~ ____	$x = 4 + 5$ $x = 9$
		pears	5 pounds	Total: __x__	
b)	Elise biked 47 km on Monday. She biked 54 km on Tuesday. How far did Elise bike in two days?	distance on Monday		Difference: ____	
				Total: ____	
c)	Alice raised $32 for charity. Ben raised $9 less than Alice. How much money did Ben raise?			Difference: ____	
				Total: ____	
d)	The Empire State Building in New York City is 1,250 ft tall. That is 200 ft shorter than the Willis Tower in Chicago. How tall is the Willis Tower?			Difference: ____	
				Total: ____	
e)	The cafeteria sold 350 cartons of milk. 198 of them were cartons of white milk. The rest were chocolate milk. How many cartons of chocolate milk did the cafeteria sell?			Difference: ____	
				Total: ____	
f)	Alexa bought 3 liters of apple juice. She bought 2 more liters of apple juice than plum juice. How much plum juice did she buy?			Difference: ____	
				Total: ____	

Operations and Algebraic Thinking 4-32

2. The world's tallest tree is about 116 m tall. The Horseshoe Falls at Niagara Falls is about 51 m tall. How much taller is the tallest tree than the Horseshoe Falls?

3. Solve each problem. Use your answer from i) as data for ii).

    a) i) Tom bought 9 hockey cards and 6 baseball cards. How many cards did he buy altogether?

       ii) Tom gave away 5 cards. How many does he have left?

    b) There are 24 players on a hockey team, and 15 of them are boys.

       i) How many girls are on the team?

       ii) How many more boys than girls are on the team?

4. Solve the two-step problems.

    a) Sarah bought 8 red jelly beans and 5 white jelly beans. She ate 4 of them. How many jelly beans does she have left?

    b) Mark downloaded 7 music files. He downloaded 3 more music files than video files. How many files did he download altogether?

    c) Raymond had $32. He bought a book, a magazine, and a CD (see pictures). How much money does he have left?

 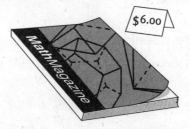 

$7.00 $6.00 $9.00

5. Nico invited 10 girls and 8 boys to his birthday party.

    a) How many more girls than boys (including Nico himself) were supposed to be at the party?

    b) Two girls and three boys could not come to the party. How many children were at the party?

    c) Were there more boys or more girls at the party? How many more?

6. The table shows the number of cars arriving at the train station parking lot. No cars leave the lot in the morning.

    a) How many cars are parked in the lot at 7:00 a.m.?

    b) How many cars are parked in the lot at 8:00 a.m.?

    c) There are 1,008 spaces in total in the lot. How many are still available at 8:00 a.m.?

Before 6:00 a.m.	378
From 6:00 a.m. to 7:00 a.m.	459
From 7:00 a.m. to 8:00 a.m.	125

OA4-33 Problems with Diagrams

1. Use the diagrams below to answer the questions about some of the tallest statues in the world.

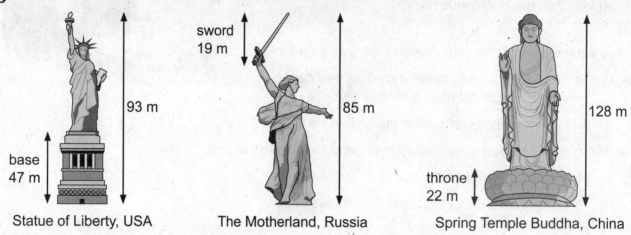

Statue of Liberty, USA   The Motherland, Russia   Spring Temple Buddha, China

a) Which is taller: the Statue of Liberty without the base or The Motherland without the sword?

b) How much taller is the Spring Temple Buddha without the throne than the whole Statue of Liberty?

c) How much taller is the Spring Temple Buddha without the throne than the whole statue of The Motherland?

d) The Statue of Liberty opened in 1886. The Motherland was built 81 years later, and the Spring Temple Buddha was built 35 years after The Motherland. When was the Spring Temple Buddha built?

2. Use the diagrams below to answer the questions about the Golden Gate Bridge in San Francisco, CA.

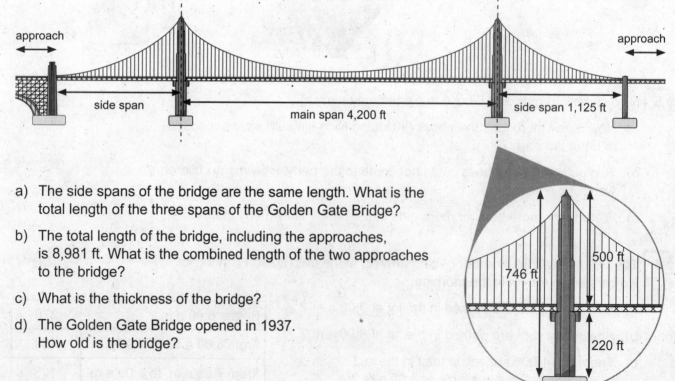

a) The side spans of the bridge are the same length. What is the total length of the three spans of the Golden Gate Bridge?

b) The total length of the bridge, including the approaches, is 8,981 ft. What is the combined length of the two approaches to the bridge?

c) What is the thickness of the bridge?

d) The Golden Gate Bridge opened in 1937. How old is the bridge?

OA4-34 Models and Times as Many

1. Draw a model for each story.

   a) Scott has 5 stamps. Jackie has 3 times as many as Scott does.

   Scott's stamps: | 5 |

   Jackie's stamps: | 5 | 5 | 5 |

   b) There are 3 red grapes. There are 5 times as many green grapes.

   _____

   _____

   c) There are 16 green pears. There are 4 times as many red pears as green pears.

   _____

   _____

   d) Ann has 4 markers. Chu has 5 times as many markers.

   _____

   _____

2. Solve each problem by drawing a model.

   a) Rocco has 6 stamps. Jen has 3 times as many stamps as Rocco.
      How many stamps do they have altogether?

   Rocco's stamps: | 6 | 6 stamps

   Jen's stamps: | 6 | 6 | 6 | 18 stamps

   $6 + 18 = 24$, so Jen and Rocco have 24 stamps altogether.

   b) Marco studies spiders and scorpions. He has 6 spiders and twice as many
      scorpions. How many critters does he have altogether?

   _____

   _____

   c) There are 4 hamsters in a store. There are six times as many mice in the store.
      How many mice and hamsters are there altogether?

3. Draw a model for each story.

a) Rina has four times as many stickers as Ilan.

   Rina's stickers: _____ | | | | |

   Ilan's stickers: _____ | |

b) Mary is three times as old as Andrew.

   _____

   _____

c) There are five times as many green grapes as red grapes.

   _____

   _____

d) A book is two times thicker than a notebook.

   _____

   _____

e) There are three times as many lizards as snakes in the zoo.

   _____

   _____

4. Draw a model for each story. Then write the given number beside the correct bar.

a) There are 20 carrots. There are 4 times as many carrots as potatoes.

   carrots: 20 _____ | | | | |

   potatoes: _____ | |

b) There are 30 cars in a parking lot. There are 6 times as many cars as vans in the lot.

   _____

   _____

c) Mona decorated her house with 70 sparkling balls and twice as many stars.

   _____

   _____

Operations and Algebraic Thinking 4-34

5. Draw the model.

a) Andrew needs three times as many blueberries as raspberries to make jam. He needs 6 cups more blueberries than raspberries. He needs 12 cups of berries altogether.

blueberries: _____

raspberries: _____

b) Dean's building is 5 times as tall as Sheila's. Dean's building is 20 floors taller than Sheila's.

_____

_____

c) There are 3 times as many green apples as red apples. There are 20 apples altogether.

_____

_____

d) There are twice as many apricots as peaches. There are 32 more apricots than peaches.

_____

_____

6. All blocks are the same size. What is the size of each block?

a)
| 5 | 5 | 5 | 5 |

| 5 | 15 |

b)

20

c)

total: 24

d)

total: 30

e)

18

f)

total: 42

7. Draw the model. Find the length of one block in the model. Then solve the problem.

a) Neil has four times as many stickers as Ali. Neil has 15 more stickers than Ali. How many stickers does each boy have?

Neil's stickers:
| 5 | 5 | 5 | 5 |

Ali's stickers:
| 5 | 15

Neil has __20__ stickers, and Ali has __5__ stickers.

b) Natasha is three times as old as Mahmud. Natasha is 8 years older than Mahmud. How old are Natasha and Mahmud?

_____

_____

Natasha is _____ years old, and Mahmud is _____ years old.

c) There are five times as many green apples as red apples. There are 24 apples altogether. How many apples of each color are there?

_____

_____

There are _____ green apples and _____ red apples.

d) A granola recipe calls for four times as much oatmeal as nuts. Bella wants to make 24 ounces of granola. How many ounces of nuts and oatmeal does she need?

_____

_____

Bella needs _____ ounces of oatmeal and _____ ounces of nuts.

e) A rottweiler weighs five times as much as a Scottish terrier. The Scottish terrier weighs 36 kg less than the rottweiler. How much does each dog weigh?

_____

_____

The Scottish terrier weighs _____ kg, and the rottweiler weighs _____ kg.

f) A pair of pants costs twice as much as a shirt. Fred paid $42 for a pair of pants and a shirt. How much did each item cost?

BONUS ▶ How much would Fred pay for two pairs of pants and three shirts?

OA4-35 Equations with Multiplication and Division

When the larger part is 3 times the size of the smaller part, we say the **scale factor** is 3.

Smaller Part ☐

Larger Part ☐☐☐

You can find one part from another part using the scale factor.

Larger Part = Smaller Part × Scale Factor

Smaller Part = Larger Part ÷ Scale Factor

1. Circle the larger part and underline the smaller part.
   Then fill in the blanks for the equation where the unknown is by itself.

   a) There are 21 cats and w dogs. There are three times as many (dogs) as cats.

   _____ = _____ × _____   or   _____ = _____ ÷ _____
   Larger Part   Smaller Part   Scale Factor   Smaller Part   Larger Part   Scale Factor

   b) There are 6 plums and w pears. There are 2 times as many plums as pears.

   _____ = _____ × _____   or   _____ = _____ ÷ _____
   Larger Part   Smaller Part   Scale Factor   Smaller Part   Larger Part   Scale Factor

   c) There are 8 boys and w girls. There are 4 times as many girls as boys.

   _____ = _____ × _____   or   _____ = _____ ÷ _____
   Larger Part   Smaller Part   Scale Factor   Smaller Part   Larger Part   Scale Factor

   d) There are 12 boys in a chess club. There are twice as many girls as boys in the chess club.

   _____ = _____ × _____   or   _____ = _____ ÷ _____
   Larger Part   Smaller Part   Scale Factor   Smaller Part   Larger Part   Scale Factor

2. Fill in the table. Write w for the number you are not given.
   Hint: Circle the larger part and underline the smaller part to write the equation.

	Problem	Part	How Many?	Equation
a)	There are 20 green apples in a box. There are 4 times as many (green apples) as red apples.	green apples	20	$20 \div 4 = w$
		red apples	w	
b)	There are 16 pears. There are twice as many pears as bananas.			
c)	There are 6 cats in a shelter. There are three times as many dogs as cats in the shelter.			
d)	Mia planted 40 bean seeds. That is 5 times as many as the corn seeds she planted. How many corn seeds did she plant?			

3. In each row of the table below some information is missing. Multiply or divide to find the missing information.

	Total Number of Things	Number of Sets	Number in Each Set	Multiplication or Division Equation
a)	w	6	3	$6 \times 3 = w$
b)	20	4	w	$20 \div 4 = w$
c)	18	w	6	
d)	24	2	w	
e)	w	4	7	

4. Fill in the chart. Write w to show what you don't know. Then write a multiplication or division equation in the last column.

		Total Number of Things	Number of Sets	Number in Each Set	Multiplication or Division Equation
a)	32 people 4 vans	32	4	w	$32 \div 4 = w$ __8__ people in each van
b)	10 marbles in each jar 6 jars				_____ _____ marbles
c)	35 flowers 5 pots				_____ _____ flowers in each pot
d)	6 chairs at each table 7 tables				_____ _____ chairs

5. a) A soccer league has 8 teams with 11 players each. How many players are in the league?

b) A maple tree is 35 feet tall. A pine tree is twice as tall the maple. How tall is the pine tree?

c) Mira is 35 years old. Mira is 5 times older than Ken. How old is Ken?

d) A box of pencils costs $2. How much do 25 boxes of pencils costs?

e) Dana paid $15 for three scarves. If all scarves cost the same, how much did each one cost?

BONUS ▶ A male mountain gorilla weighs 440 pounds, four times as much as a male chimpanzee. How much does the chimpanzee weigh?

Operations and Algebraic Thinking 4-35

OA4-36 More Totals and Differences (Advanced)

1. Fill in the table.

Problem	Parts	How Many?	Scale Factor / Difference
a) There are 20 green apples in a box. There are 4 times as many (green apples) as red apples.	green apples	20	Scale Factor: ___4___
	red apples	x	~~Difference:~~
b) Five people can ride in a car. Eight times as many people can ride on a bus.	people in a car		Scale Factor: _____
			Difference: _____
c) There are 16 pears. There are twice as many pears as plums.			Scale Factor: _____
			Difference: _____
d) A table costs $120. A desk costs $30 more than the table.			Scale Factor: _____
			Difference: _____
e) A bed is 210 cm long, and a desk is 100 cm shorter than the bed.			Scale Factor: _____
			Difference: _____
f) There are 15 cars in the parking lot and 5 more vans than cars.			Scale Factor: _____
			Difference: _____
g) Ariel is twice as old as Helen. Ariel is 12 years old.			Scale Factor: _____
			Difference: _____
h) Jennifer is 3 years old. Ron is 5 years older than Jennifer.			Scale Factor: _____
			Difference: _____

2. Calculate the total for each problem in Question 1. If you do not know the difference, calculate that too.

3. A store sold 6 rats and twice as many hamsters.

   a) How many hamsters did the store sell?

   b) How many rats and hamsters were sold altogether?

   c) How many more hamsters than rats were sold?

4. Ms. A's Class has twice as many boys as girls. There are 18 boys in the class.

   a) How many girls are in the class?

   b) How many students are in the class?

   c) How many more boys than girls are in the class?

5. Nina read that an hour of doing aerobics burns 300 calories and an hour of hockey burns 100 calories more. How many calories would she burn doing aerobics for an hour and then playing hockey for an hour?

6. A recreation pass costs $22 and is $10 more than a movie pass. How much do the two passes cost together?

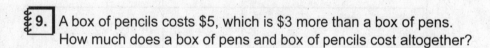

7. A bookstore sold 120 books on Friday and twice as many books on Saturday. On Sunday the store sold 50 more books than on Saturday.

   a) How many books did the store sell on Saturday and on Sunday?

   b) How many more books did the store sell on Sunday than on Friday?

   c) How many books did the store sell over the three days?

8. Karen weighs 93 pounds. She is three times as heavy as her dog Binky. How much do Karen and Binky weigh together? How many more pounds does Karen weigh than Binky?

9. A box of pencils costs $5, which is $3 more than a box of pens. How much does a box of pens and box of pencils cost altogether?

10. Ellen is 5 times as old as George. Ellen is 35. How much older than George is Ellen?

11. A female angler fish is 5 times as large as a male angler fish. The female can be 100 cm long. How much longer than the male is the female angler fish?

OA4-37 Comparisons (Advanced)

1. Write the equation.

   a) 8 is 4 times as many as 2.

   _____$8 = 4 \times 2$_____

   c) 7 is 5 fewer than 12.

   _____

   e) 18 is twice as many as 9.

   _____

   b) 12 is 3 more than 9.

   _____$12 = 9 + 3$_____

   d) 12 is 4 times as much as 3.

   _____

   f) 6 is 3 times as much as 2.

   _____

2. Fill in the missing number.

   a) 18 is __9__ times as many as 2.

   c) 7 is _____ fewer than 18.

   e) 16 is _____ times as many as 2.

   b) 12 is _____ more than 6.

   d) 18 is _____ times as much as 3.

   f) 24 is _____ times as much as 4.

3. a) Juliette read 6 pages. Romeo read 18 pages. How many times as many pages did Romeo read as Juliette? _____

   b) Five people can ride in a car, and eight people can ride in a van. How many more people can ride in the van than in the car? _____

   c) Forty people can ride on a bus, and eight people can ride in a van. How many times as many people can ride on the bus as in the van? _____

4. a) The Tigers beat the Flyers 6–3. How many times as many goals did the Tigers score as the Flyers? _____

   b) The Hurricanes beat the Storms 8–2. How many times as many goals did the Hurricanes score as the Storms? _____

   c) How many more goals did the Hurricanes score than the Tigers? _____

   d) How many goals in total were scored at both games together? _____

5. a) Jane has 5 more crayons than Bob. Bob has 4 crayons.

Bob:

Jane:

How many crayons do they have altogether? _____

b) Jane has 5 times as many crayons as Bob. Bob has 4 crayons.

Bob:

Jane:

How many crayons do they have altogether? _____

c) How are parts a) and b) the same? How are they different?

6. Draw a picture for the situation.

a) There are three times as many red apples as green apples. There are twice as many yellow apples as green apples.

red apples:

green apples:

yellow apples:

b) There are four times as many cats as dogs. There are twice as many hamsters as dogs.

cats:

dogs:

hamsters:

c) A hat costs 4 times as much as a pair of mitts. A scarf costs twice as much as the hat.

mitts:

hat:

scarf:

d) A bus is 3 times as long as a car. The bus is 6 times as long as a bike.

car:

bus:

bike:

7. Draw a picture to solve the problem.

   a) Rob has twice as many crayons as Tara. Marco has five times as many crayons as Tara. Tara has 3 crayons. How many more crayons does Marco have than Rob?

   Tara:

   Rob:

   Marco:

   Answer: Marco has _____ more crayons than Rob.

   b) Dara's pencil is twice as long as Mark's and 3 cm longer than Carrie's. Mark's pencil is 5 cm long. How long is Carrie's pencil?

   c) A pencil is two times as long as an eraser. A book is five times as long as the eraser. The book is 12 cm longer than the pencil. How long is each object?

   d) A pair of pants costs twice as much as a shirt. The shirt costs three times as much as a pair of socks. Alwyn paid $40 for the pants, the shirt, and the pair of socks. How much did each item cost?

A dog weighs three times as much as a cat. An iguana weighs 4 kg less than the dog.

Emily drew a picture for this situation. She does not know how many white blocks long the bar for the iguana's weight should be, so she drew it a different color.

Cat's weight
Dog's weight
Iguana's weight   4 kg

---

8. Draw a picture to solve the problem.

   a) A scarf costs twice as much as a hat. The hat costs $15. A pair of mitts costs $10 less than the scarf. How much do the hat, the scarf, and the mitts cost together?

   _____

   _____

   _____

   Answer: _____

   b) Javier is four times as old as Kong. Kong is 3 years younger than Ewa. Javier is 9 years older than Ewa. How old is each person? Hint: Draw Ewa's bar in the middle.

OA4-38 Multistep Word Problems

1. a) There are 12 blue beads. There are 3 times as many blue beads as red beads.
   There are 7 fewer yellow beads than blue beads.

   How many red beads are there? _____   How many yellow beads are there? _____

   b) Ron is 3 times older than Jo. Karen is four years older than Jo. Jo is 6 years old.

   How old is Ron? _____   How old is Karen? _____

2. Diana is two years older than Farhad. Farhad is 10 years old. Farhad is 7 years older
   than Chen. How old are Diana and Chen?

   Diana is _____ years old and Chen is _____ years old.

3. Daniel bought six books about mammals and two books about reptiles.
   Each book cost $12.

   a) How many books did Daniel buy altogether? _____

   b) How much did the books cost? _____

4. Noah bought 7 books and 10 magazines. (See the prices in the picture.)

   a) How much did Noah spend on books? _____

   b) How much did Noah spend on magazines? _____

   c) How much did Noah spend altogether? _____

   Sale!
   $12 $15
   Books   Magazines

5. What question do you need to ask and answer before you can solve the problem?

   a) Maya has twice as many hockey cards as Ron does. Maya has 10 more hockey
      cards than Henry. Henry has 16 hockey cards. How many cards does Ron have?

      How many cards does Maya have? _____

   b) Bob is twice as old as Miki. Miki is three years older than Nomi.
      Nomi is five years old. How old is Bob?

      _____

   c) Rani had $53. She spent $15 on a hat, $8 on a scarf, and $12 on a pair of mitts.
      How much money does Rani have left?

      _____

6. Tanya earns $15 per hour. She worked 3 hours on Friday, 2 hours on Saturday,
   and 2 hours on Sunday. How much money did Tanya earn in these three days?

7. Aya used 3 times as many blue beads as red beads for a bracelet. She used 12 more blue beads than yellow beads. She used 3 yellow beads.

   a) How many beads of each color did Aya use?

   b) How many beads did she use in total?

8. Snow geese can fly 100 miles in 2 hours. They can fly for a very long time.

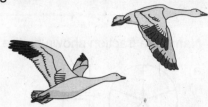

   a) Some snow geese flew for 18 hours, rested, and then flew for another 20 hours. How long did the geese travel? How far did the geese travel?

   b) Snow geese need to fly about 3,000 miles from Alaska to Texas. How much flying time do the geese need?

9. A narwhal is an arctic whale. The adult male has one very long tooth. An adult narwhal is about 16 feet long from nose to tail, and its tooth is 9 feet long. Use the diagram to tell how long a baby narwhal is.

adult male narwhal

baby narwhal

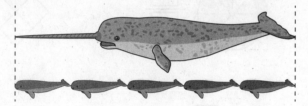

10. An eraser is 2 inches long. A pencil is 6 inches long. Write your answer as a full sentence.

   a) How many times longer is the pencil than the eraser?

   b) How many inches longer is the pencil than the eraser?

11. An elephant weighs 13,000 pounds and is 13 feet tall. Is this elephant 1,000 times heavier than it is tall? Explain.

12. There are 5 people at a pizza party. They ordered 2 pizzas. Each pizza has 8 slices. Each person gets the same number of slices. How many slices can each person have?

13. There are 52 avocados in a crate. Thirteen are spoiled. Tim packs the rest into bags of 5 avocados. How many bags can he make?

14. There are 24 students in one class and 23 students in another class going on a field trip. Each car can hold 4 students. How many cars are needed to transport all the students?

NF4-1 Naming Fractions

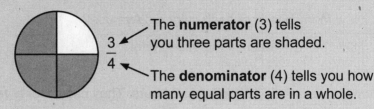
1. Name the fraction shown by the shaded part of each image.

   a) 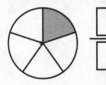 $\frac{1}{5}$

   b) $\frac{1}{4}$

   c) $\frac{1}{6}$

   d) $\frac{6}{9}$

   e) 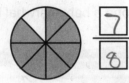 $\frac{7}{8}$

   f)  $\frac{3}{10}$

2. Shade the fractions named.

   a) $\frac{1}{6}$

   b) $\frac{1}{5}$

   c) $\frac{1}{9}$

   d) $\frac{3}{6}$

   e) $\frac{2}{5}$

   f) $\frac{5}{9}$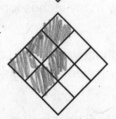

3. Use one of the following words to describe each square in the figures below.

   half   third   fourth   fifth   sixth   seventh   eighth   ninth

   a)

   b)

   c)

   _____   _____   _____

1. Which strip has more shaded? Circle its fraction.

a)  $\frac{2}{3}$

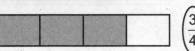 $\left(\frac{3}{4}\right)$

b) 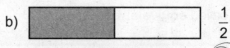 $\frac{1}{2}$

 $\left(\frac{5}{6}\right)$

c) 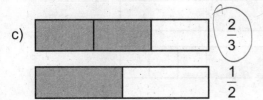 $\left(\frac{2}{3}\right)$

$\frac{1}{2}$

d)  $\frac{1}{4}$

$\left(\frac{3}{8}\right)$

e) 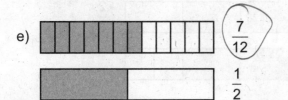 $\left(\frac{7}{12}\right)$

$\frac{1}{2}$

f) 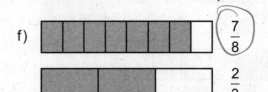 $\left(\frac{7}{8}\right)$

$\frac{2}{3}$

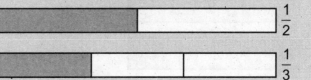

$\frac{1}{2}$ is **greater than** $\frac{1}{3}$ because more is shaded. $\frac{1}{2}$

$\frac{1}{3}$

2. Shade the amounts. Circle the greater fraction.

a)  $\frac{2}{3}$

 $\left(\frac{5}{6}\right)$

b) 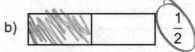 $\left(\frac{1}{2}\right)$

 $\frac{3}{8}$

c)  $\left(\frac{10}{12}\right)$

$\frac{3}{4}$

d) 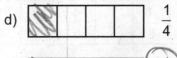 $\frac{1}{4}$

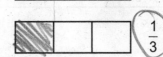 $\left(\frac{1}{3}\right)$

"5 is greater than 3" is written 5 > 3.   "3 is less than 5" is written 3 < 5.

3. Write your answers to Question 2 using < or >.

a) $\frac{2}{3}$ ☐ $\frac{5}{6}$ b) $\frac{1}{2}$ ☐ $\frac{3}{8}$ c) $\frac{10}{12}$ ☐ $\frac{3}{4}$ d) $\frac{1}{4}$ ☐ $\frac{1}{3}$

One third **equals** two sixths because
the same amount is shaded.

$\frac{1}{3}$ and $\frac{2}{6}$ are called **equivalent** fractions.

4. Complete the equivalent fractions.

a) $\frac{1}{2} = \frac{2}{4}$

b) $\frac{1}{2} = \frac{3}{6}$

c) $\frac{1}{3} = \frac{2}{6}$

d) $\frac{2}{3} = \frac{4}{6}$

e) $\frac{2}{2} = \frac{10}{10}$

f) $\frac{4}{10} = \frac{2}{5}$

5. Use the picture to find the equivalent fractions.

a)

1 whole							
$\frac{1}{2}$				$\frac{1}{2}$			
$\frac{1}{4}$		$\frac{1}{4}$		$\frac{1}{4}$		$\frac{1}{4}$	
$\frac{1}{8}$	$\frac{1}{8}$	$\frac{1}{8}$	$\frac{1}{8}$	$\frac{1}{8}$	$\frac{1}{8}$	$\frac{1}{8}$	$\frac{1}{8}$

$\frac{1}{4} = \frac{2}{8}$ $\frac{1}{2} = \frac{4}{8}$

$\frac{6}{8} = \frac{3}{4}$ $\frac{2}{4} = \frac{1}{2}$

b)

1 whole									
$\frac{1}{5}$		$\frac{1}{5}$		$\frac{1}{5}$		$\frac{1}{5}$		$\frac{1}{5}$	
$\frac{1}{10}$	$\frac{1}{10}$	$\frac{1}{10}$	$\frac{1}{10}$	$\frac{1}{10}$	$\frac{1}{10}$	$\frac{1}{10}$	$\frac{1}{10}$	$\frac{1}{10}$	$\frac{1}{10}$

$\frac{1}{5} = \frac{2}{10}$ $\frac{6}{10} = \frac{3}{5}$

$\frac{4}{5} = \frac{8}{10}$ $\frac{5}{5} = \frac{10}{10}$

Number and Operations—Fractions 4-2

NF4-3 Equal Parts and Models of Fractions

1. Use a centimeter ruler to divide the line into equal parts. The first one is started for you.

   a) 5 equal parts

   b) 8 equal parts

   _____

   c) 6 equal parts

   _____

2. Using a ruler, join the marks to divide the box into equal parts.

   a) 4 equal parts

   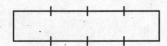

   b) 5 equal parts

   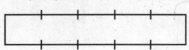

3. Mark the box in centimeters. Then divide the box into equal parts.

   a) 3 equal parts

   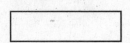

   b) 6 equal parts

4. Using a ruler, find what fraction of the box is shaded.

   a) [   ] is shaded.

   b) [   ] is shaded.

5. Using a ruler, complete the figure to make a whole.

   a) $\frac{1}{2}$

   b) $\frac{2}{3}$

6. Sketch a rectangle cut in halves. Then cut it in fourths.

7. You have $\frac{3}{8}$ of a pie.

   a) What does the bottom (denominator) of the fraction tell you?

   b) What does the top (numerator) of the fraction tell you?

8. Explain why each picture does (or does not) show $\frac{1}{4}$.

   a)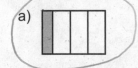

   b)

   c)

   d)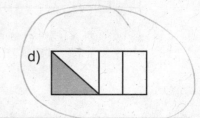

NF4-4 Fractions on Number Lines

We can use number lines instead of fraction strips to show fractions.

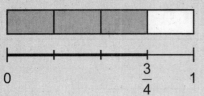

$\frac{3}{4}$ of the strip is shaded.

$\frac{3}{4}$ of the number line from 0 to 1 is shaded.

1. Find what fraction of the number line from 0 to 1 is shaded.

a)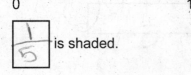

$\boxed{\frac{1}{5}}$ is shaded.

So $\boxed{\frac{2}{5}}$ is shaded.

b)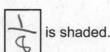

$\boxed{\frac{1}{8}}$ is shaded.

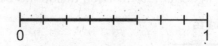

So $\boxed{\frac{5}{8}}$ is shaded.

To find $\frac{3}{4}$ on a number line, divide the number line from 0 to 1 into **4** equal parts.

Then start at 0 and take **3** parts.

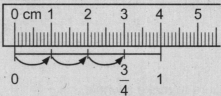

2. Use a ruler to divide the number line from 0 to 1 into equal parts, and then mark the fraction.

a) 3 equal parts and mark $\frac{1}{3}$

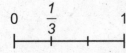

b) 5 equal parts and mark $\frac{2}{5}$

c) 6 equal parts and mark $\frac{3}{6}$

d) 8 equal parts and mark $\frac{6}{8}$

Number and Operations—Fractions 4-4

3. Pamela marks $\frac{3}{4}$ on the number line. John marks $\frac{2}{3}$ on the same number line.

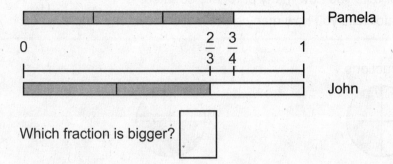

Pamela

John

Which fraction is bigger? ☐

You can use number lines to compare fractions.

$\frac{3}{4}$ is greater than $\frac{2}{4}$ because it is farther to the right: $\frac{3}{4} > \frac{2}{4}$.

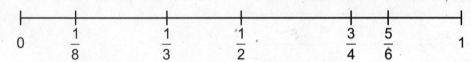

---

4. Anna placed fractions with different denominators on the same number line.

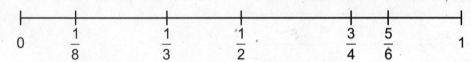

a) Write $<$ (less than) or $>$ (greater than).

i) $\frac{1}{8}$ ☐ $\frac{1}{2}$ ii) $\frac{3}{4}$ ☐ $\frac{1}{3}$ iii) $\frac{5}{6}$ ☐ $\frac{3}{4}$

b) Circle these fractions on the number line above. Then write them from greatest to least.

$\frac{1}{2}, \frac{5}{6}, \frac{1}{3}$ > >

Two fractions are equivalent if they mark the same place on a number line from 0 to 1.

---

5. Use the number lines to find equivalent fractions.

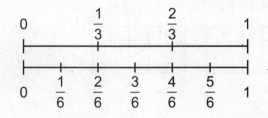

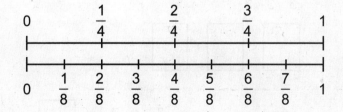

a) $\frac{1}{3} = \frac{2}{6}$ b) $\frac{2}{3} = \frac{4}{6}$ c) $\frac{1}{4} = \frac{2}{8}$ d) $\frac{3}{4} = \frac{6}{8}$

NF4-5 More Comparing Fractions

> **REMINDER ▶** $\frac{3}{8}$ ← The numerator tells you how many parts are counted.
>
> ← The denominator tells you how many equal parts are in one whole.

1. a) Write the numerators of the shaded fractions.

 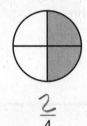 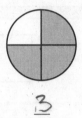

$$\frac{1}{4} \qquad\qquad \frac{2}{4} \qquad\qquad \frac{3}{4}$$

b) Look at the pictures and fractions in part a). Write "increases," "decreases," or "stays the same."

   i) The numerator ___incresed___ .

   ii) The denominator ___stays same___ .

   iii) The fraction shaded ___increseise___ .

Same number of parts in one whole   and   *more parts shaded* ⟶ *more shaded*

same denominator   and   *larger numerator* ⟶ *greater fraction*

$\frac{3}{5} > \frac{2}{5}$ because 3 fifths is more than 2 fifths.

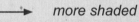
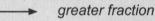

---

2. Circle the greater fraction in each pair.

a) $\frac{3}{8}$ or $\boxed{\frac{6}{8}}$ b) $\boxed{\frac{7}{12}}$ or $\frac{4}{12}$ c) $\boxed{\frac{5}{10}}$ or $\frac{2}{10}$ **BONUS ▶** $\boxed{\frac{74}{85}}$ or $\frac{69}{85}$

3. Write the fractions in order from least to greatest.

a) $\frac{2}{3}, \frac{1}{3}, \frac{3}{3}$

$\boxed{\frac{1}{3}} < \boxed{\frac{2}{3}} < \boxed{\frac{3}{3}}$

b) $\frac{2}{10}, \frac{1}{10}, \frac{7}{10}, \frac{9}{10}$

$\boxed{\frac{1}{10}} < \boxed{\frac{2}{10}} < \boxed{\frac{7}{10}} < \boxed{\frac{9}{10}}$

4. Write a fraction between $\frac{3}{8}$ and $\frac{7}{8}$. $\boxed{\frac{6}{8}}$

5. a) What fraction of a cup is in the container?

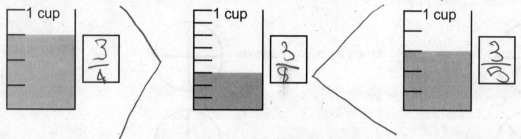

b) Place the fractions from part a) in order from least to greatest.

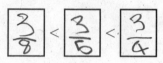

c) Write "bigger" or "smaller":

As the denominator (bottom) of the fraction gets bigger, each part gets _Smaller_.

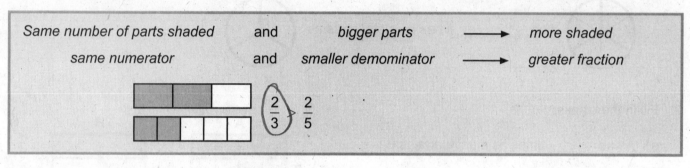

Same number of parts shaded   and   bigger parts   →   more shaded

same numerator   and   smaller demominator   →   greater fraction

$\dfrac{2}{3}$ > $\dfrac{2}{5}$

6. Circle the greater fraction in each pair.

a) $\dfrac{1}{5}$ or $\dfrac{1}{6}$

b) $\dfrac{3}{10}$ or $\dfrac{3}{8}$

c) $\dfrac{5}{12}$ or $\dfrac{5}{10}$

BONUS ▶ $\dfrac{93}{100}$ or $\dfrac{93}{1,000}$

7. Write the fractions in order from least to greatest.

a) $\dfrac{1}{5}, \dfrac{1}{2}, \dfrac{1}{4}$

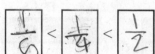

b) $\dfrac{4}{6}, \dfrac{4}{8}, \dfrac{4}{10}, \dfrac{4}{9}$

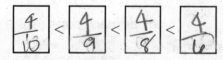

8. Write a fraction between $\dfrac{2}{9}$ and $\dfrac{2}{3}$.

9. a) Two fractions have the same *numerators* (tops) but different *denominators* (bottoms). How can you tell which fraction is greater?

b) Two fractions have the same *denominators* (bottoms) but different *numerators* (tops). How can you tell which fraction is greater?

Number and Operations—Fractions 4-5

NF4-6 Equivalent Fractions and Multiplication

1. How many times as many parts?

a)  has ___2___ times as many parts as

b) has ___4___ times as many parts as

c) has ___3___ times as many parts as

d) has ___2___ times as many parts as

2. Fill in the blanks.

a) A has ___2___ times as many parts as B.

A has ___2___ times as many shaded parts as B.

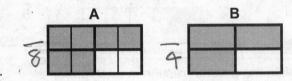

b) A has ___8___ times as many parts as B.

A has ___4___ times as many shaded parts as B.

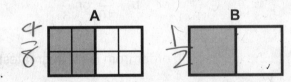

c) A has ___4___ times as many parts as B.

A has ___4___ times as many shaded parts as B.

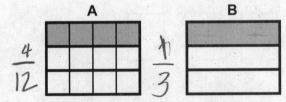

d) A has ___3___ times as many parts as B.

A has ___3___ times as many shaded parts as B.

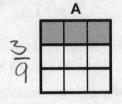

     Number and Operations—Fractions 4-6

3. The picture shows two equivalent fractions. Fill in the blanks.

a)  $\dfrac{1}{5}$ and $\dfrac{2}{10}$

2 is ___2___ times as much as 1.

10 is ___2___ times as much as 5.

b) 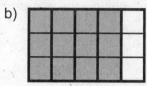 $\dfrac{4}{5}$ and $\dfrac{12}{15}$

12 is ___3___ times as much as 4.

15 is ___3___ times as much as 5.

c)  $\dfrac{1}{4}$ and $\dfrac{2}{8}$

2 is ___2___ times as much as 1.

8 is ___2___ times as much as 4.

d) 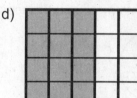 $\dfrac{3}{5}$ and $\dfrac{12}{20}$

12 is ___4___ times as much as 3.

20 is ___4___ times as much as 5.

4. Write an equivalent fraction for the picture. Then write how many times as much the new numerator and denominator are.

a) 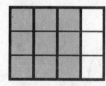 $\dfrac{3}{4} = \boxed{\dfrac{9}{12}}$

___3___ times as much

b) $\dfrac{1}{4} = \boxed{\dfrac{4}{16}}$

___4___ times as much

c)  $\dfrac{3}{5} = \boxed{\dfrac{6}{10}}$

___2___ times as much

BONUS ▶

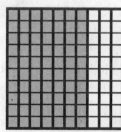 $\dfrac{7}{10} = \boxed{\dfrac{}{100}}$

_____ times as much

To get an equivalent fraction, multiply the numerator and denominator by the same number.

Example:　Picture A 　　$\dfrac{3}{4} \xrightarrow[\times 2]{\times 2} \dfrac{6}{8}$　　Picture B

Picture B has twice as many **parts** as Picture A.
Picture B has twice as many **shaded parts** as Picture A.

5. Draw lines to cut the pies into more equal pieces. Then fill in the numerators of the equivalent fractions.

a)

   4 pieces   6 pieces   8 pieces

$\dfrac{1}{2} = \dfrac{}{4} = \dfrac{}{6} = \dfrac{}{8}$

b)

   6 pieces   9 pieces   12 pieces

$\dfrac{1}{3} = \dfrac{}{6} = \dfrac{}{9} = \dfrac{}{12}$

6. Cut each pie into more pieces. Then fill in the missing numbers.

a) 　$\dfrac{2}{3} \xrightarrow[\times 2]{\times 2} \dfrac{}{6}$

b) 　$\dfrac{3}{4} \xrightarrow[\times 2]{\times 2} \dfrac{}{8}$

c) 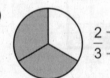　$\dfrac{2}{3} \xrightarrow[\times]{\times} \dfrac{}{9}$

This number tells you how many pieces to cut each slice into.

7. Use multiplication to find the equivalent fraction.

a) $\dfrac{1 \times 2}{3 \times 2} = \dfrac{}{6}$ b) $\dfrac{1 \times }{2 \times } = \dfrac{}{10}$ c) $\dfrac{2}{5} = \dfrac{}{10}$

d) $\dfrac{3}{4} = \dfrac{}{8}$ e) $\dfrac{1}{4} = \dfrac{}{12}$ f) $\dfrac{4}{5} = \dfrac{}{15}$

g) $\dfrac{5}{6} = \dfrac{}{12}$ h) $\dfrac{3}{10} = \dfrac{}{100}$ i) $\dfrac{5}{9} = \dfrac{}{72}$

8. Write five fractions equivalent to $\dfrac{7}{10}$.

$\dfrac{7}{10} = \boxed{} = \boxed{} = \boxed{} = \boxed{} = \boxed{}$

1. Name the shaded fraction.

a)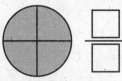

b)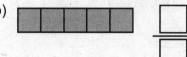

2. A fraction is equivalent to 1 if its numerator and denominator are _____.

Ron ate more than one whole pizza! Each pizza had four equal slices, and Ron ate 5 slices:

Ron ate $\frac{5}{4}$ of a pizza.

3. Write if the fraction is "more" or "less" than 1.

a)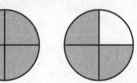

$\frac{7}{4}$ is _____ than 1.

b)

$\frac{5}{8}$ is _____ than 1.

4. A fraction is greater than 1. Which is greater, the numerator or denominator?

_____

5. Write "more" or "less."

$1 = \frac{8}{8}$ so $\frac{9}{8}$ is _____ than 1.

$1 = \frac{5}{5}$ so $\frac{4}{5}$ is _____ than 1.

So $\frac{9}{8}$ is _____ than $\frac{4}{5}$.

6. Lina thinks that $\frac{4}{3}$ is less than $\frac{99}{100}$ because the numbers are smaller. Is she right? _____

Explain how you know. _____

_____

7. Circle the fractions that are more than half.

$\frac{3}{4}$ $\qquad$ $\frac{3}{5}$ $\qquad$ $\frac{3}{6}$ $\qquad$ $\frac{3}{7}$ $\qquad$ $\frac{3}{8}$

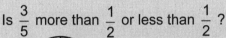

Is $\frac{3}{5}$ more than $\frac{1}{2}$ or less than $\frac{1}{2}$?

3 parts are shaded, and $5 - 3 = 2$ parts are not shaded.

More parts are shaded than not shaded, so $\frac{3}{5} > \frac{1}{2}$.

8. How many shaded parts does the fraction show? How many parts are not shaded?

a) $\frac{5}{12}$ _____ shaded

_____ not shaded

b) $\frac{3}{8}$ _____ shaded

_____ not shaded

c) $\frac{4}{7}$ _____ shaded

_____ not shaded

9. Write $>$ or $<$.

a) $\frac{2}{5}$ ☐ $\frac{1}{2}$ b) $\frac{4}{9}$ ☐ $\frac{1}{2}$ c) $\frac{6}{11}$ ☐ $\frac{5}{12}$ d) $\frac{13}{25}$ ☐ $\frac{1}{2}$ e) $\frac{23}{50}$ ☐ $\frac{1}{2}$ f) $\frac{5}{11}$ ☐ $\frac{1}{2}$

10. Write "more" or "less."

a) $\frac{4}{6}$ is _____ than $\frac{1}{2}$.

$\frac{1}{4}$ is _____ than $\frac{1}{2}$.

So $\frac{4}{6}$ is _____ than $\frac{1}{4}$.

b) $\frac{4}{9}$ is _____ than $\frac{1}{2}$.

$\frac{53}{100}$ is _____ than $\frac{1}{2}$.

So $\frac{4}{9}$ is _____ than $\frac{53}{100}$.

11. Karen ate $\frac{3}{8}$ of a pizza. Is that more or less than half the pizza? _____

12. In a Fourth Grade class, $\frac{5}{7}$ of the students are girls. Are there more girls or boys in the class?

13. On a baseball team, $\frac{5}{11}$ of the players are girls. Are there more girls or boys on the team?

14. Quentin ate $\frac{3}{5}$ of a pizza, and Jasmine ate $\frac{1}{3}$ of the pizza. Who ate more pizza?

NF4-8 Comparing Fractions Using Equivalent Fractions

1. Draw lines to cut the pies into more equal pieces. Then fill in the numerators of the equivalent fractions.

   a)

   $\frac{2}{3} = \frac{4}{6} = \frac{6}{9} = \frac{8}{12} = \frac{}{15}$

   $\frac{2}{3} \times \frac{2}{2} = \frac{4}{6}$

   $\frac{2}{3} \times \frac{3}{3} = \frac{6}{9}$

   $\frac{2}{3} \times \frac{4}{4} = \frac{8}{12}$

   b)

   $\frac{3}{5} = \frac{}{10} = \frac{}{15} = \frac{}{20} = \frac{}{25}$

2. a) Write two fractions with the same denominator. Hint: Use your answers from Question 1.

   $\frac{2}{3} = \boxed{}$ and $\frac{3}{5} = \boxed{}$

   b) Which of the two fractions is greater, $\frac{2}{3}$ or $\frac{3}{5}$? _____ $\frac{2}{3}$

   0.667 0.6

   How do you know? _____

   _____

3. Rewrite the fractions so that they have the same denominator. Then circle the larger fraction.

   a) $\frac{1 \times 5}{3 \times 5} = \frac{5}{15}$ and $\frac{2 \times 3}{5 \times 3} = \boxed{\frac{10}{15}}$

   b) $\frac{3 \times 3}{8 \times 3} = \boxed{\frac{9}{24}}$ and $\frac{1 \times 8}{3 \times 8} = \frac{8}{24}$

4. a) Write an equivalent fraction with denominator 12.

   i) $\frac{2 \times 4}{3 \times 4} = \frac{8}{12}$ ii) $\frac{5}{6 \times 2} = \frac{10}{12}$ iii) $\frac{3 \times 3}{4 \times 3} = \frac{9}{12}$ iv) $\frac{1 \times 6}{2 \times 6} = \frac{6}{12}$

   b) Write the fractions from part a) in order from least to greatest.

    < < <

5. Draw lines to cut the left-hand pie into the same number of equal pieces as the right-hand pie. Complete the equivalent fraction. Then circle the greater fraction.

a)

$$\frac{1}{2} = \frac{}{4} \qquad \frac{1}{4}$$

b)

$$\frac{2}{3} = \frac{}{6} \qquad \frac{5}{6}$$

6. Turn the fraction on the left into an equivalent fraction with the same denominator as the fraction on the right. Then write < (less than) or > (greater than) to show which fraction is greater.

a) $\dfrac{1 \times 3}{2 \times 3} = \dfrac{3}{6}$ ⬛ $\dfrac{4}{6}$

b) $\dfrac{1 \times 4}{2 \times 4} = \dfrac{4}{8}$ ⬛ $\dfrac{5}{8}$

c) $\dfrac{1 \times 2}{2 \times 2} = \dfrac{2}{4}$ ⬛ $\dfrac{3}{4}$

d) $\dfrac{1 \times 3}{3 \times 3} = \dfrac{3}{9}$ ⬛ $\dfrac{2}{9}$

e) $\dfrac{1 \times 2}{5 \times 2} = \dfrac{2}{10}$ ⬛ $\dfrac{7}{10}$

f) $\dfrac{1 \times 4}{4 \times 4} = \dfrac{4}{16}$ ⬛ $\dfrac{3}{16}$

Pedro wants to turn $\dfrac{1}{3}$ and $\dfrac{2}{5}$ into fractions with the same denominator.

He multiplies the denominators together: $3 \times 5 = 5 \times 3$.

$$\dfrac{5 \times 1}{5 \times 3} \text{ and } \dfrac{2 \times 3}{5 \times 3}$$

$$= \dfrac{5}{15} \qquad = \dfrac{6}{15} \qquad \dfrac{5}{15} < \dfrac{6}{15}, \text{ so } \dfrac{1}{3} < \dfrac{2}{5}$$

7. Turn the fractions into fractions with the same denominator. Then compare the fractions. Show your answer using < or >.

a) $\dfrac{7 \times 3}{7 \times 4} \quad \dfrac{5 \times 4}{7 \times 4}$

$= \dfrac{21}{28} \quad = \dfrac{20}{28}$

so $\dfrac{3}{4}$ ⬛ $\dfrac{5}{7}$

b) $\dfrac{\times 1}{\times 2} \quad \dfrac{2 \times}{3 \times}$

$= \dfrac{}{} \quad = \dfrac{}{}$

so $\dfrac{1}{2}$ ⬛ $\dfrac{2}{3}$

c) $\dfrac{\times 1}{\times 2} \quad \dfrac{3 \times}{4 \times}$

$= \dfrac{}{} \quad = \dfrac{}{}$

so $\dfrac{1}{2}$ ⬛ $\dfrac{3}{4}$

d) $\dfrac{\times 2}{\times 3} \quad \dfrac{5 \times}{8 \times}$

$= \dfrac{}{} \quad = \dfrac{}{}$

so $\dfrac{2}{3}$ ⬛ $\dfrac{5}{8}$

8. Draw a picture to justify your answer to Question 7 c).

Number and Operations—Fractions 4-8

NF4-9 Problems and Puzzles (Advanced)

> How much is in half depends on how much is in the whole.

1. John and Anna each ate $\frac{1}{2}$ a pizza.

   Who ate more pizza? _____

   Anna's pizza   John's pizza

2. Is $\frac{1}{4}$ of Figure 1 the same size as $\frac{1}{4}$ of Figure 2?

   Explain why or why not. _____

   _____

   Figure 1   Figure 2

3. a) Which picture can be used to compare $\frac{1}{2}$ and $\frac{3}{5}$? _____

   A.    B.   C.

   b) Why can't you use the other ones? _____

   _____

   c) Which is greater: $\frac{1}{2}$ or $\frac{3}{5}$? _____ How do you know? _____

   _____

4. What fraction of the whole is a single triangle?

   a)  ___   b)  ___   c)  ___   d) 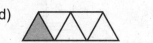 ___

5. Look at your answers to Question 4. Write "bigger" or "smaller."

   The triangle is a bigger fraction of a _____ whole.

6. Is it possible for $\frac{1}{4}$ of a pie to be bigger than $\frac{1}{2}$ of another pie?

   Show your thinking with a picture.

7. Use centimeters and millimeters to write a fraction equivalent to $\frac{2}{3}$.

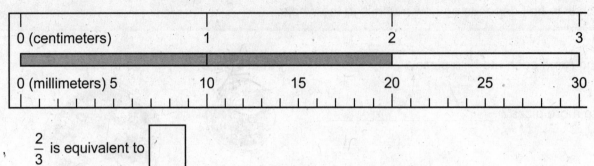

$\frac{2}{3}$ is equivalent to ⬜

8. Use the number lines to write a fraction equivalent to $\frac{2}{6}$.

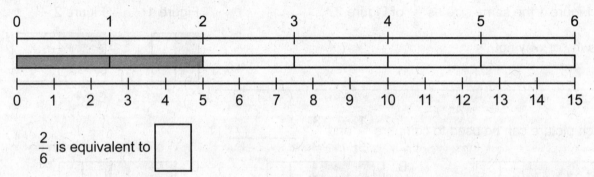

$\frac{2}{6}$ is equivalent to ⬜

9. Use two of 2, 3, 4, and 5 to create …

a) the least possible fraction.

b) a fraction greater than 1.

c) a fraction equivalent to $\frac{1}{2}$.

10. Use each digit exactly once to make three correct statements. Cross out the digits as you use them.

a) 1   2̸   3   4   5   6   7   8̸

$\frac{1}{4} = \dfrac{\boxed{2}}{\boxed{8}}$ $\frac{1}{2} = \dfrac{\square}{\square}$ $\dfrac{\square}{\square} < \dfrac{\square}{\square}$

b) 1   2   3   4   5   6

$\frac{1}{2} < \dfrac{\square}{\square} < 1$ $\dfrac{\square}{\square} < \frac{1}{2}$ $\dfrac{\square}{\square} > 1$

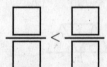
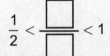

📓 **BONUS ▶** Find more ways to answer Question 10.

Number and Operations—Fractions 4-9

NF4-10 Adding Fractions

1. Tom took one piece from each pizza. Combine the pieces onto one plate.
   What fraction of a pizza did he take?

   a)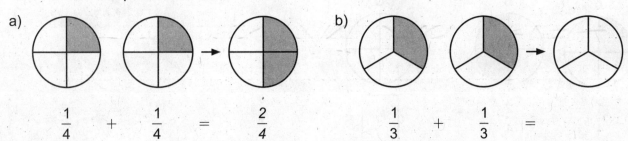

   $$\frac{1}{4} \quad + \quad \frac{1}{4} \quad = \quad \frac{2}{4}$$

   b)

   $$\frac{1}{3} \quad + \quad \frac{1}{3} \quad =$$

   c)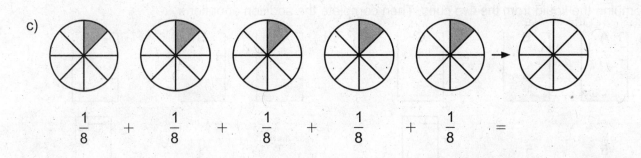

   $$\frac{1}{8} \quad + \quad \frac{1}{8} \quad + \quad \frac{1}{8} \quad + \quad \frac{1}{8} \quad + \quad \frac{1}{8} \quad =$$

   > Since $1 + 1 + 1 = 3$, so 1 fifth + 1 fifth + 1 fifth = 3 fifths.
   > $$\frac{1}{5} \quad + \quad \frac{1}{5} \quad + \quad \frac{1}{5} \quad = \quad \frac{3}{5}$$

2. Add. Then write the addition equation.

   a) 1 fifth + 1 fifth = ___2___ fifths

   $$\frac{1}{5} \quad + \quad \frac{1}{5} \quad = \quad \frac{2}{5}$$

   b) 1 eighth + 1 eighth = _____ eighths

   c) 1 third + 1 third + 1 third + 1 third = _____ thirds

3. Add.

   a) $\frac{1}{3} + \frac{1}{3} =$

   b) $\frac{1}{5} + \frac{1}{5} + \frac{1}{5} + \frac{1}{5} + \frac{1}{5} + \frac{1}{5} =$

   c) $\frac{1}{8} + \frac{1}{8} + \frac{1}{8} + \frac{1}{8} + \frac{1}{8} + \frac{1}{8} + \frac{1}{8} =$

   d) $\frac{1}{7} + \frac{1}{7} + \frac{1}{7} + \frac{1}{7} =$

4. Write the fraction as a sum of fractions with numerator 1.

   a) $\frac{4}{5} =$

   b) $\frac{3}{2} =$

NF4-11 Adding and Subtracting Fractions

1. Combine the pieces of pie onto one plate. Then write a fraction for the part you shaded.

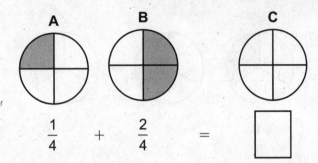

$$\frac{1}{4} \quad + \quad \frac{2}{4} \quad = \quad \boxed{}$$

2. Combine the liquid from the two cups. Then complete the addition equations.

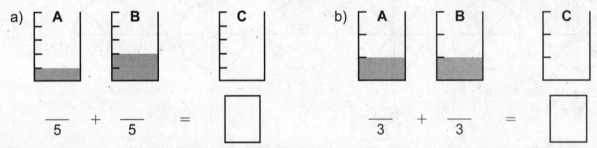

a) $\dfrac{}{5} + \dfrac{}{5} = \boxed{}$

b) $\dfrac{}{3} + \dfrac{}{3} = \boxed{}$

3. Add.

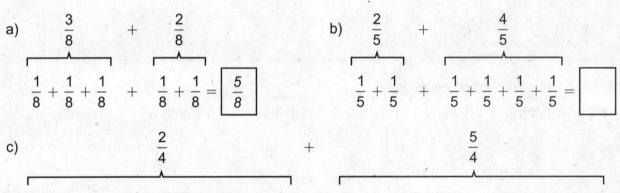

a) $\dfrac{3}{8} + \dfrac{2}{8}$

$$\frac{1}{8} + \frac{1}{8} + \frac{1}{8} \quad + \quad \frac{1}{8} + \frac{1}{8} = \boxed{\frac{5}{8}}$$

b) $\dfrac{2}{5} + \dfrac{4}{5}$

$$\frac{1}{5} + \frac{1}{5} \quad + \quad \frac{1}{5} + \frac{1}{5} + \frac{1}{5} + \frac{1}{5} = \boxed{}$$

c) $\dfrac{2}{4} \quad + \quad \dfrac{5}{4}$

$$= \boxed{}$$

4. Write the addition equation.

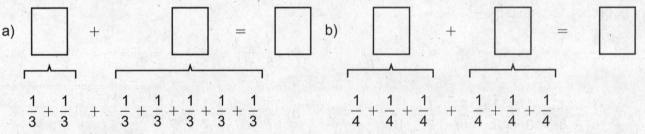

a) $\boxed{} + \boxed{} = \boxed{}$

$$\frac{1}{3} + \frac{1}{3} \quad + \quad \frac{1}{3} + \frac{1}{3} + \frac{1}{3} + \frac{1}{3} + \frac{1}{3}$$

b) $\boxed{} + \boxed{} = \boxed{}$

$$\frac{1}{4} + \frac{1}{4} + \frac{1}{4} \quad + \quad \frac{1}{4} + \frac{1}{4} + \frac{1}{4}$$

5. Add the fractions.

a) $\dfrac{3}{5} + \dfrac{3}{5} =$ b) $\dfrac{2}{4} + \dfrac{1}{4} =$ c) $\dfrac{3}{7} + \dfrac{6}{7} =$ d) $\dfrac{5}{8} + \dfrac{2}{8} =$

6. Subtract by taking away the second amount.

a) $\dfrac{5}{4} - \dfrac{2}{4} = \boxed{\dfrac{3}{4}}$

$\dfrac{1}{4} + \dfrac{1}{4} + \dfrac{1}{4} + \boxed{\dfrac{1}{4} + \dfrac{1}{4}}$ ↗

b) $\dfrac{5}{8} - \dfrac{3}{8} = \boxed{}$

$\dfrac{1}{8} + \dfrac{1}{8} + \boxed{\dfrac{1}{8} + \dfrac{1}{8} + \dfrac{1}{8}}$ ↗

c) $\dfrac{7}{5} - \dfrac{4}{5} = \boxed{}$

$\dfrac{1}{5} + \dfrac{1}{5} + \dfrac{1}{5} + \dfrac{1}{5} + \dfrac{1}{5} + \dfrac{1}{5} + \dfrac{1}{5}$

d) $\dfrac{4}{3} - \dfrac{2}{3} = \boxed{}$

Break $\dfrac{4}{3}$ into thirds. Then take away $\dfrac{2}{3}$.

7. Subtract.

a) $\dfrac{2}{3} - \dfrac{1}{3} =$

b) $\dfrac{3}{5} - \dfrac{2}{5} =$

c) $\dfrac{6}{7} - \dfrac{3}{7} =$

d) $\dfrac{11}{5} - \dfrac{3}{5} =$

8. Mark ate $\dfrac{3}{10}$ of a pizza and Sarah ate $\dfrac{4}{10}$ of the pizza.

a) What fraction of the pizza did they eat altogether? $\boxed{}$

b) Write the equation that shows your answer to a).

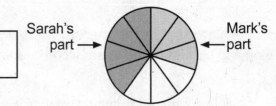
Sarah's part → ← Mark's part

_____

9. Pedro ate $\dfrac{2}{8}$ of a pie and Noreen ate $\dfrac{3}{8}$ of the pie.

a) Use the picture to show how much each person ate.

b) What fraction of the pie did they eat altogether?

c) Write the equation that shows your answer to b).

10. Katya ate $\dfrac{3}{5}$ of a pie. Roman ate the rest.

a) Use the picture to show how much each person ate.

b) Write an equation that shows how much Roman ate.

11. Angela adds $\dfrac{4}{10} + \dfrac{1}{10}$. She says her answer is equal to $\dfrac{1}{2}$. Is she right? Explain.

NF4-12 Improper Fractions and Mixed Numbers (Introduction)

Alan and his friends ate **9** quarter-sized pieces of pizza.

Altogether they ate $\frac{9}{4}$ pizzas.

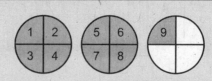

When the numerator of a fraction is larger than the denominator, the fraction represents **more than** one whole. Such fractions are called **improper fractions**.

1. Write an improper fraction for each picture.

   a)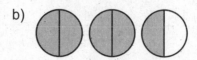

   b)

2. Shade one piece at a time until you have shaded the amount of pie given.

   a) $\frac{5}{2}$

   b) $\frac{7}{2}$

   c) $\frac{8}{3}$

   d) $\frac{13}{4}$

Alan and his friends ate two and one quarter pies (or $2\frac{1}{4}$ pies):

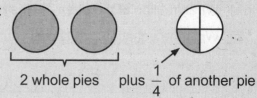

$2\frac{1}{4}$ is called a **mixed number** because it is a mixture of a whole number and a fraction.

2 whole pies   plus $\frac{1}{4}$ of another pie

3. Write how many **whole** pies are shaded.

   a)

   __2__ whole pies

   b)

   _____ whole pies

   c)

   _____ whole pie

4. Write the fraction as a mixed number.

   a)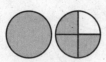

   _____

   b)

5. Shade the amount of pie given. There may be more pies in the picture than you need.

a) $2\frac{1}{2}$

b) $3\frac{2}{3}$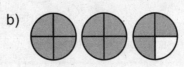

6. Write these fractions as mixed numbers and as improper fractions.

a)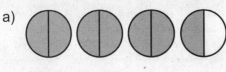

$\boxed{} = \boxed{}$

b)

$\boxed{} = \boxed{}$

c)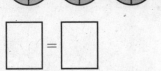

$\boxed{} = \boxed{}$

d)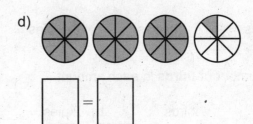

$\boxed{} = \boxed{}$

7. Write a mixed number and an improper fraction for the number of cups.

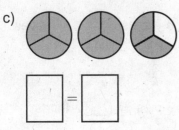

1 cup   1 cup   1 cup

mixed number $\boxed{}$ improper fraction $\boxed{}$

8. Shade the amount of pie given. Then write an improper fraction for the amount of pie.

a) $2\frac{1}{2}$ 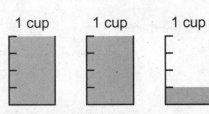 $\boxed{}$

b) $3\frac{1}{4}$ 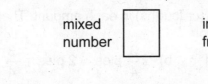 $\boxed{}$

9. Shade the amount of pie given. Then write a mixed number for the amount of pie.

a) $\frac{7}{3}$ 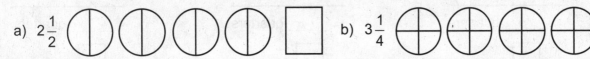 $\boxed{}$

b) $\frac{13}{6}$ 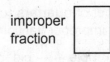 $\boxed{}$

10. Sketch the pies. Then write an equivalent mixed number or improper fraction.

a) $2\frac{1}{2}$ pies   b) $\frac{9}{2}$ pies   c) $\frac{10}{4}$ pies   d) $3\frac{2}{3}$ pies

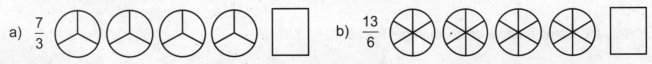

NF4-13 Improper Fractions and Mixed Numbers

How many quarter pieces are in $2\frac{1}{4}$ pies?

     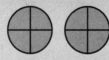   

4 quarters   8 (= 2 × 4) quarters   8 quarters + 1 extra quarter = 9 quarters

So there are 9 quarter-sized pieces altogether.

1. Find the number of **halves** in each amount.

   a) 1 pie = _____ halves

   b) 2 pies = _____ halves

   c) 3 pies = _____ halves

   $1\frac{1}{2}$ pies = _____ halves

   $2\frac{1}{2}$ pies = _____ halves

   $3\frac{1}{2}$ pies = _____ halves

2. Find the number of **thirds** in each amount.

   a) 1 pie = _____ thirds

   b) 2 pies = _____ thirds

   c) 3 pies = _____ thirds

   $1\frac{1}{3}$ pies = _____ thirds

   $2\frac{2}{3}$ pies = _____ thirds

   $3\frac{1}{3}$ pies = _____ thirds

3. Find the number of **quarters** (or fourths) in each amount. Then write the mixed number as an improper fraction.

   a) $1\frac{1}{4}$ pies = 1 pie + $\frac{1}{4}$ pie

   b) $2\frac{3}{4}$ pies = 2 pies + $\frac{3}{4}$ pies

   c) $3\frac{2}{4}$ pies = 3 pies + $\frac{2}{4}$ pies

   a) = ___4___ quarters

   + ___1___ quarter

   = ___5___ quarters

   = $\dfrac{5}{4}$

   b) = _____ quarters

   = _____ quarters

   = _____ quarters

   = $\dfrac{\boxed{}}{\boxed{}}$

   c) = _____ quarters

   = _____ quarters

   = _____ quarters

   = $\dfrac{\boxed{}}{\boxed{}}$

4. Write the mixed number as an improper fraction.

   a) $3\frac{1}{4} =$ b) $3\frac{4}{5} =$ c) $5\frac{1}{2} =$ d) $2\frac{1}{5} =$ e) $5\frac{2}{3} =$ f) $7\frac{3}{10} =$

5. Pens come in packs of 8. Dan used $1\frac{5}{8}$ packs. How many pens did he use? _____

6. Bottles come in packs of 6. How many bottles are in $2\frac{5}{6}$ packs? _____

7. Circle groups that equal 1. Then write the improper fraction as a mixed number.

a) $\dfrac{7}{3} = \boxed{\dfrac{1}{3} + \dfrac{1}{3} + \dfrac{1}{3}} + \boxed{\dfrac{1}{3} + \dfrac{1}{3} + \dfrac{1}{3}} + \dfrac{1}{3} = 2\dfrac{1}{3}$

b) $\dfrac{9}{2} = \boxed{\dfrac{1}{2} + \dfrac{1}{2}} + \boxed{\dfrac{1}{2} + \dfrac{1}{2}} + \boxed{\dfrac{1}{2} + \dfrac{1}{2}} + \boxed{\dfrac{1}{2} + \dfrac{1}{2}} + \dfrac{1}{2} =$

c) $\dfrac{11}{4} = \dfrac{1}{4} + \dfrac{1}{4} + \dfrac{1}{4} + \dfrac{1}{4} + \dfrac{1}{4} + \dfrac{1}{4} + \dfrac{1}{4} + \dfrac{1}{4} + \dfrac{1}{4} + \dfrac{1}{4} + \dfrac{1}{4} =$

d) $\dfrac{11}{3} = \dfrac{1}{3} + \dfrac{1}{3} + \dfrac{1}{3} + \dfrac{1}{3} + \dfrac{1}{3} + \dfrac{1}{3} + \dfrac{1}{3} + \dfrac{1}{3} + \dfrac{1}{3} + \dfrac{1}{3} + \dfrac{1}{3} =$

e) $\dfrac{12}{5} = \dfrac{1}{5} + \dfrac{1}{5} + \dfrac{1}{5} + \dfrac{1}{5} + \dfrac{1}{5} + \dfrac{1}{5} + \dfrac{1}{5} + \dfrac{1}{5} + \dfrac{1}{5} + \dfrac{1}{5} + \dfrac{1}{5} + \dfrac{1}{5} =$

How many wholes are in $\dfrac{9}{4}$? A whole is 4 quarters, so make groups of 4:

$\dfrac{9}{4} = \boxed{\dfrac{1}{4} + \dfrac{1}{4} + \dfrac{1}{4} + \dfrac{1}{4}} + \boxed{\dfrac{1}{4} + \dfrac{1}{4} + \dfrac{1}{4} + \dfrac{1}{4}} + \dfrac{1}{4} = 2\dfrac{1}{4}$

There are 2 groups of four quarters, and 1 quarter is left over. Since $9 \div 4 = 2$ R 1, then $\dfrac{9}{4} = 2\dfrac{1}{4}$.

---

8. Find the number of wholes in each amount by dividing.

a) $\dfrac{4}{2} = $ _____ wholes

b) $\dfrac{6}{2} = $ _____ wholes

c) $\dfrac{10}{2} = $ _____ wholes

9. Write the improper fraction as a mixed number by dividing.

a) $\dfrac{9}{2}$

$9 \div 2 = $ _____ R _____

So $\dfrac{9}{2} = \boxed{}$

b) $\dfrac{15}{4}$

$15 \div 4 = $ _____ R _____

So $\dfrac{15}{4} = \boxed{}$

c) $\dfrac{22}{5}$

$22 \div 5 = $ _____ R _____

So $\dfrac{22}{5} = \boxed{}$

d) $\dfrac{14}{5} =$ e) $\dfrac{68}{10} =$ f) $\dfrac{32}{3} =$ g) $\dfrac{30}{8} =$ h) $\dfrac{40}{7} =$ i) $\dfrac{28}{7} =$

NF4-14 Adding and Subtracting Mixed Numbers

1. How many halves are in each amount?

a) $3\frac{1}{2} + 4\frac{1}{2}$ $(3 \times 2) + 1$

   $= \underline{\quad 7 \quad}$ halves $+ \underline{\quad 9 \quad}$ halves

   $= \underline{\quad 16 \quad}$ halves

b) $5 + 1\frac{1}{2}$

   $= \underline{\qquad}$ halves $+ \underline{\qquad}$ halves

   $= \underline{\qquad}$ halves

c) $6\frac{1}{2} - 2$

   $= \underline{\qquad}$ halves $- \underline{\qquad}$ halves

   $= \underline{\qquad}$ halves

d) $4 - 1\frac{1}{2}$

   $= \underline{\qquad}$ halves $- \underline{\qquad}$ halves

   $= \underline{\qquad}$ halves

2. How many thirds are in each amount?

a) $7\frac{1}{3} + 2\frac{1}{3}$

   $= \underline{\qquad}$ thirds $+ \underline{\qquad}$ thirds

   $= \underline{\qquad}$ thirds

b) $8\frac{1}{3} - 2\frac{2}{3}$

   $= \underline{\qquad}$ thirds $- \underline{\qquad}$ thirds

   $= \underline{\qquad}$ thirds

3. Add or subtract. Write your answer two ways. One answer will be a whole number.

a) $1\frac{3}{8} + 2\frac{4}{8} = \frac{11}{8} + \frac{20}{8}$

   $= \boxed{\dfrac{31}{8}}$ ← improper fraction

   $= \boxed{3\dfrac{7}{8}}$ ← mixed number

b) $6\frac{7}{10} - 2\frac{4}{10} = \dfrac{\quad}{10} - \dfrac{\quad}{10}$

   $= \boxed{}$ ← improper fraction

   $= \boxed{}$ ← mixed number

c) $1 + 5\frac{3}{4}$ d) $1\frac{5}{8} + 2\frac{3}{8}$ e) $6 - 2\frac{3}{5}$ f) $7\frac{1}{8} - 3\frac{4}{8}$

4. Rima needs $1\frac{2}{5}$ cups of flour to make a cake and 2 cups of flour to make a pizza.

How much flour does she need altogether? $\underline{\qquad}$

5. Mike bought a rope $2\frac{1}{4}$ feet long. He cut off $\frac{3}{4}$ of a foot from it. How much rope is left? $\underline{\qquad}$

NF4-15 Equal Parts of a Set

Fractions can name parts of a set: $\frac{1}{5}$ of the figures are squares, $\frac{1}{5}$ are circles, and $\frac{3}{5}$ are triangles.

1. Fill in the blanks.

a)

☐ of the figures are circles.

☐ of the figures are shaded.

b)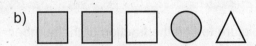

☐ of the figures are shaded.

☐ of the figures are triangles.

2.

a) $\frac{4}{8}$ of the figures are _____.

b) $\frac{3}{8}$ of the figures are _____.

3. A soccer team wins 5 games and loses 3 games.

a) How many games did the team play? ☐

b) What fraction of the games did the team win? ☐

4. A box contains 4 blue markers, 3 black markers, and 3 red markers. What fraction of the markers are *not* blue?

5. Write four fraction statements for the picture: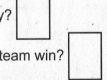

6. Draw a picture that fits all the clues.

a) There are 5 circles and squares.

$\frac{3}{5}$ of the figures are squares.

$\frac{2}{5}$ of the figures are shaded.

Two circles are shaded.

b) There are 5 triangles and squares.

$\frac{3}{5}$ of the figures are shaded.

$\frac{2}{5}$ of the figures are triangles.

One square is shaded.

NF4-16 Fractions of Whole Numbers

Dan has 6 cookies.

He wants to give $\frac{1}{3}$ of his cookies to a friend.

He makes 3 equal groups and gives 1 group to his friend.

There are 2 cookies in each group, so $\frac{1}{3}$ of 6 is 2.

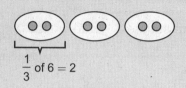

1. Use the picture to find the fraction of the number.

   a)
   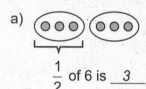

   $\frac{1}{2}$ of 6 is ___3___

   b)

   $\frac{1}{3}$ of 12 is _____

   c)
   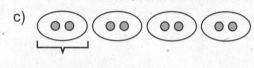

   _____ of 8 is _____

   d)

   _____ of 8 is _____

Tia has 10 cookies. She wants to give $\frac{3}{5}$ of her cookies to a friend. She makes 5 equal groups and gives 3 of the groups to her friend.

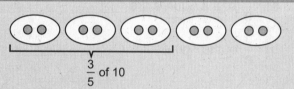

There are 2 in each group. So there are 6 in 3 groups. So $\frac{3}{5}$ of 10 is 6.

---

2. Circle the given amount.

   a) $\frac{2}{3}$ of 6

   b) $\frac{3}{4}$ of 8

   c) $\frac{4}{5}$ of 10

   d) $\frac{3}{4}$ of 12
   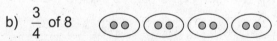

3. Draw the correct number of dots in each group, and then circle the given amount.

   a) $\frac{2}{3}$ of 12

   b) $\frac{2}{3}$ of 9

4. Draw a picture to find $\frac{3}{4}$ of 12 cookies.

Number and Operations—Fractions 4-16

Gerome finds $\frac{1}{3}$ of 6 by dividing: 6 divided into 3 equal groups gives 2 in each group.

 $6 \div 3 = 2$ So $\frac{1}{3}$ of 6 is 2.

5. Find the fraction of the number. Write the division you used in the box.

a) $\frac{1}{2}$ of 8 = ___4___   b) $\frac{1}{2}$ of 10 = _____   c) $\frac{1}{2}$ of 16 = _____   d) $\frac{1}{2}$ of 20 = _____

| $8 \div 2$ | | | |

e) $\frac{1}{3}$ of 9 = _____   f) $\frac{1}{3}$ of 15 = _____   **BONUS▶** $\frac{1}{1,000}$ of 4,000 = _____

6. Circle $\frac{1}{2}$ of each set of lines. Hint: Count the lines and divide by 2.

a) | | | | | | b) | | | | | | | | |

c) | | | | | | | | | | | | d) | | | | | | | | | | | | |

7. Shade $\frac{1}{3}$ of the circles. Then circle $\frac{2}{3}$.

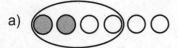

a) ◉◉○○○○   b) ○○○○○○○○○○○○

c) ○○○   d) ○○○○○○○ ○○○○○○○

8. Shade $\frac{1}{4}$ of the triangles. Then circle $\frac{3}{4}$.

9. Shade $\frac{3}{5}$ of the boxes. Hint: First count the boxes and find $\frac{1}{5}$.

a)    b)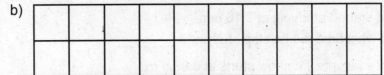

Andy finds $\frac{2}{3}$ of 12 as follows:

Step 1: He finds $\frac{1}{3}$ of 12 by dividing 12 by 3: 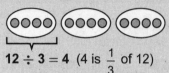 **Step 2:** He multiplies the result by 2: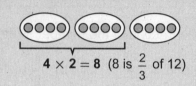

$12 \div 3 = 4$ (4 is $\frac{1}{3}$ of 12) $4 \times 2 = 8$ (8 is $\frac{2}{3}$ of 12)

10. Find the following amounts using Andy's method.

a) $\frac{2}{3}$ of 9

$\frac{1}{3}$ of 9 is _____

So $\frac{2}{3}$ of 9 is _____

b) $\frac{3}{4}$ of 8

$\frac{1}{4}$ of 8 is _____

So $\frac{3}{4}$ of 8 is _____

c) $\frac{2}{3}$ of 15

$\frac{1}{3}$ of 15 is _____

So $\frac{2}{3}$ of 15 is _____

d) $\frac{2}{5}$ of 10

$\frac{1}{5}$ of 10 is _____

So $\frac{2}{5}$ of 10 is _____

e) $\frac{3}{5}$ of 25

_____

f) $\frac{2}{7}$ of 14

_____

g) $\frac{1}{6}$ of 18

_____

h) $\frac{1}{2}$ of 12

_____

i) $\frac{3}{4}$ of 12

_____

j) $\frac{2}{3}$ of 21

_____

k) $\frac{3}{8}$ of 16

_____

l) $\frac{3}{7}$ of 21

_____

11. Five children are on a bus. $\frac{3}{5}$ are girls. How many girls are on the bus? _____

12. A pound of plums costs \$8. How much would $\frac{3}{4}$ of a pound cost? _____

13. Gerald has 12 apples. He gave away $\frac{3}{4}$ of the apples. How many did he keep?

14. Ed studied for $\frac{2}{3}$ of an hour.

a) How many minutes did he study for? _____

b) Ed started studying at 7:10 p.m.
At what time did he stop studying? _____

c) Ed's favorite TV show starts at 8:00 p.m.
Did he finish studying before the show started? _____

NF4-17 Multiplying a Fraction by a Whole Number

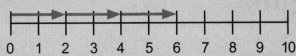

Remember: You can multiply whole numbers on a number line.

3 arrows of length 2 gives a total length of:

$$2 + 2 + 2 = 3 \times 2 = 6$$

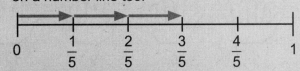

You can multiply fractions on a number line too.

3 arrows of length $\frac{1}{5}$ gives a total length of:

$$\frac{1}{5} + \frac{1}{5} + \frac{1}{5} = 3 \times \frac{1}{5} = \frac{3}{5}$$

1. Multiply using the number line.

a)

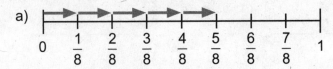

$5 \times \frac{1}{8} =$

b)

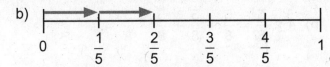

$2 \times \frac{1}{5} =$

c)

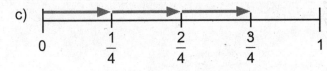

$3 \times \frac{1}{4} =$

d)

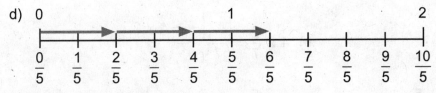

$3 \times \frac{2}{5} = \frac{6}{5}$

e)

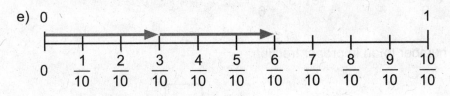

$2 \times \frac{3}{10} =$

2. Draw arrows above and below the number line to multiply the fraction.

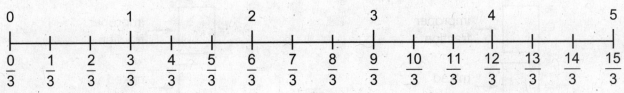

a) $2 \times \frac{4}{3} =$

b) $6 \times \frac{2}{3} =$

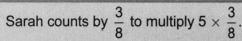

Sarah counts by $\frac{3}{8}$ to multiply $5 \times \frac{3}{8}$.

$\frac{3}{8}$ $\frac{6}{8}$ $\frac{9}{8}$ $\frac{12}{8}$ $\frac{15}{8}$ So $5 \times \frac{3}{8} = \frac{15}{8} = 1\frac{7}{8}$

3. Multiply by skip counting. Change your answer to a mixed number.

a) $5 \times \frac{3}{7}$ $\frac{3}{7}$, $\frac{6}{7}$, ___ , ___ , ___   So $5 \times \frac{3}{7} =$ ___ = ___ ___

b) $5 \times \frac{2}{9}$ ___ , ___ , ___ , ___ , ___   So $5 \times \frac{2}{9} =$ ___ = ___ ___

4. Multiply by adding.

a) $3 \times \frac{4}{5} = \frac{4}{5} + \frac{4}{5} + \frac{4}{5} =$

b) $4 \times \frac{5}{8} = \frac{5}{8} + \frac{5}{8} + \frac{5}{8} + \frac{5}{8} =$

c) $8 \times \frac{3}{7} = \frac{3}{7} + \frac{3}{7} + \frac{3}{7} + \frac{3}{7} + \frac{3}{7} + \frac{3}{7} + \frac{3}{7} + \frac{3}{7} =$

5. Multiply mentally.

a) $5 \times \frac{3}{8} = \frac{\boxed{15}}{8}$ ← 5×3

b) $4 \times \frac{2}{7} = \frac{\boxed{}}{7}$ ← 4×2

c) $2 \times \frac{4}{9} =$ d) $5 \times \frac{5}{9} =$ e) $3 \times \frac{5}{6} =$ f) $2 \times \frac{5}{3} =$

6. Multiply by changing the mixed number to an improper fraction.
Write your answer two ways.

a) $4 \times 1\frac{2}{5} = 4 \times \boxed{}$

= $\boxed{}$ ← improper fraction

= $\boxed{}$ ← mixed number

b) $2 \times 3\frac{1}{3} = 2 \times \boxed{}$

= $\boxed{}$ ← improper fraction

= $\boxed{}$ ← mixed number

c) $3 \times 2\frac{1}{5}$ d) $5 \times 1\frac{3}{8}$ e) $7 \times 1\frac{4}{5}$ f) $2 \times 3\frac{5}{6}$

Number and Operations—Fractions 4-17

NF4-18 Problems and Puzzles

1. Five people each ate $\frac{1}{8}$ of a cake. Write an addition and a multiplication

   to show how much they ate altogether.

   Addition: _____   Multiplication: _____

2. Leo wants to make grilled cheese sandwiches for five people.

   Each person needs $\frac{3}{8}$ of a pound of cheese.

   a) How many pounds of cheese does he need? _____
      Hint: Use the picture to help.

   b) Leo has 2 pounds of cheese. Does he need to buy more cheese? _____

3. Latasha makes 5 batches of a pizza. Each batch needs $\frac{2}{3}$ cups of flour.

   a) How much flour will she need altogether? _____

   b) She has 4 cups of flour. How much flour will she have left? _____

      Hint: Shade the amount of flour she needs. How many thirds are not shaded?

4. Lee makes 8 batches of cookies for a bake sale. Each batch needs $2\frac{3}{4}$ of a cup of flour.
   A cup of flour costs 30¢. How much does he have to pay for the flour?
   Write your answer in both cents and dollars.

5. Six people are having dinner together. Each person needs $\frac{3}{8}$ of a pound of turkey.

   a) How many pounds of turkey will be needed? ☐

   b) Between what two whole numbers does your answer lie? _____ and _____

6. Sarah says $3 \times 2\frac{1}{5} = 6\frac{3}{5}$ because $3 \times 2 = 6$ and $3 \times \frac{1}{5} = \frac{3}{5}$. Is she right?

   Draw a picture to help you decide.

7. Write $\frac{7}{8}$ as a sum of two or more fractions in at least five ways.

Example: $\frac{7}{8} = \frac{1}{8} + \frac{3}{8} + \frac{3}{8}$

8. Write $\frac{1}{2}$ as a sum of three or more fractions in at least five ways.

Hint: First write some fractions that are equivalent to $\frac{1}{2}$: $\frac{2}{4}$, $\frac{3}{6}$, $\frac{4}{8}$, and so on.

9. a) Tasha wants to pour the juice from these two containers into a third container that is the same size.
Will the container overflow?

b) Is $\frac{4}{5} + \frac{1}{3}$ greater than 1? How do you know?

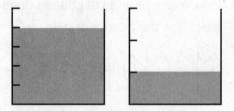

10. a) Tony had $\frac{2}{3}$ of a cup of juice. He drank $\frac{1}{3}$ of a *cup*.

Show on the picture how much he drank.
How much does he have left?

b) Alicia had $\frac{2}{3}$ of a cup of juice. She drank $\frac{1}{3}$ of the *juice*.

Use a ruler to show on the picture how much she drank.

c) Alicia says she has $\frac{1}{3}$ of a cup left because $\frac{2}{3} - \frac{1}{3} = \frac{1}{3}$.

Is she right? Explain.

Tony   **Alicia**

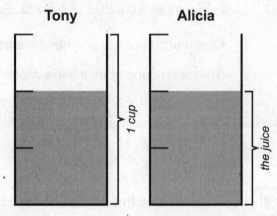

11. A flower garden has 10 flowers.

$\frac{1}{2}$ of the flowers are lilies. $\frac{2}{5}$ of the flowers are daffodils.

a) How many lilies are in the garden?

b) How many daffodils are in the garden?

c) How many flowers are either lilies or daffodils?

d) Calculate $\frac{1}{2} + \frac{2}{5}$. Hint: Use your answer to part c).

BONUS ▶ How many more lilies are there than daffodils? Use your answer to calculate $\frac{1}{2} - \frac{2}{5}$.

MD4-18 Grams and Kilograms

Mass is the amount of matter in an object. The heavier an object, the greater its mass.

1. Circle the object with the greater mass in real life.

   a) 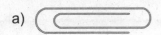   b)

2. Match each object in the top row to an object with a similar mass in the bottom row.

The mass of small objects is often measured in **grams**. We write 1 **g** for 1 gram.

A large paper clip and a chocolate chip each weigh about 1 gram.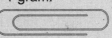

3. What is the mass of the group of objects?

   a) 2 large paper clips _____   b) 12 chocolate chips _____

4. A nickel has a mass of 5 g.

   a) What is the mass of 10 nickels? _____   50 nickels? _____

   b) What is the mass of each amount in nickels?

      i) 5¢ _____   ii) 50¢ _____   iii) 80¢ _____   iv) 100¢ _____

5. Estimate the mass of the object in grams. Measure the mass to the nearest gram.

   a) a cookie   b) an apple

      Estimate: _____   Measure: _____   Estimate: _____   Measure: _____

   c) a shoe   d) a pencil

      Estimate: _____   Measure: _____   Estimate: _____   Measure: _____

6. Write in the missing masses to balance the scales.

a)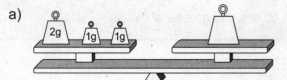

b)

Mass is also measured in **kilograms**.

A quart of orange juice has a mass of about 1 kg.

7. Circle the correct mass for the item.

a)

2 g or 2 kg

b)

15 g or 15 kg

c)

35 g or 35 kg

d)

270 g or 270 kg

8. Circle the unit that is more appropriate to measure the mass of the item.

a) pencil

g or kg

b) desk

g or kg

c) your backpack

g or kg

d) 3-year-old human

g or kg

e) moose

g or kg

f) tiny bird

g or kg

g) slice of cheese

g or kg

h) car

g or kg

9. Estimate the mass of the object in kilograms. Measure the mass to the nearest kilogram.

a) a backpack

Estimate: _____   Measure: _____

b) a large water bottle

Estimate: _____   Measure: _____

c) a pile of books

Estimate: _____   Measure: _____

d) a basketball

Estimate: _____   Measure: _____

10. Cross out the objects that weigh more than 1 kg. Circle the objects that weigh between 1 g and 1 kg.

    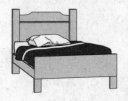

MD4-19 Changing Units of Mass

1 kilogram = 1,000 grams	1 kg = 1,000 g

1. Fill in the table.

kg	1	2	3	4	5	6	7	8
g	*1,000*							

2. Change the following measurements to grams.

a) 3 kg = _____   b) 9 kg = _____   c) 17 kg = _____   d) 25 kg = _____

3. Convert the measurement in kilograms to grams. Then circle the greater measurement.

a) 500 g (7 kg)   b) 8,300 g   95 kg   c) 24,567 g   15 kg
   7,000 g

d) 2,222 g   2 kg   e) 60 kg   6,200 g   f) 72 kg   45,203 g

4. Use the table in Question 1.

a) Write a measurement in grams that is between 5 kg and 6 kg. _____

b) Write a measurement in kilograms that is between 3,790 g and 4,258 g. _____

5. Convert the measurements in grams to mixed measurements.

a) 5,130 g = ___5___ kg ___130___ g   b) 5,217 g = _____ kg _____ g

c) 4,367 g = _____ kg _____ g   d) 4,081 g = _____ kg _____ g

e) 7,006 g = _____ kg _____ g   f) 44,300 g = _____ kg _____ g

6. Convert the mixed measurements to measurements in grams.

a) 3 kg = ___3,000___ g   b) 4 kg = _____ g   c) 5 kg = _____ g
   so 3 kg 71 g   so 4 kg 510 g   so 5 kg 45 g

	3,	0	0	0	g
+			7	1	g
	3,	0	7	1	g

=					g
+					g
					g

=					g
+					g
					g

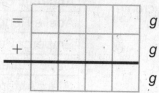
d) 8 kg 128 g = _____ g   e) 9 kg 237 g = _____ g

f) 7 kg 3 g = _____ g

Problems Involving Mass

1. ...ung raccoon weighs 2 kg. ...ow much would …

a) 3 raccoons weigh?

b) 7 raccoons weigh?

2. There are 15 salmon in a pond, and each weighs about two kilograms. About how much do all the salmon in the pond weigh?

3. A spoon weighs about 60 grams. About how much would a set of 6 spoons weigh?

4. The cost of shipping a package is $2.00 per kilogram. How much does it cost to ship a package that weighs 12 kilograms?

5. A mail carrier is carrying 300 letters in his bag. Each letter has a mass of about 20 g. What is the total mass of the letters in kilograms?

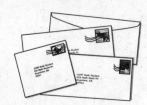

6. Tomato and eggplant seeds weigh 2 g each. Zucchini seeds weigh 3 g each.

a) Daniel bought 12 tomato seeds, 8 eggplant seeds, and 5 zucchini seeds. How much did his seeds weigh altogether?

b) Rani bought 1 kg of tomato seeds. How many seeds did she buy?

7. A male hippo weighs 1,876 kg and a female hippo weighs 1,347 kg.

a) How much less does the female weigh than the male?

b) How much do the male and the female hippos weigh together?

8. a) Baby Amanda weighs 3,547 grams. Baby Pedro weighs 4 kg. Who is heavier? Explain.

b) Jennifer weighed 3 kg at birth. She grew at a rate of 200 g each week. How much did Jennifer weigh when she was four weeks old?

9. Use the information from the table to create a word problem. Solve your problem.

Antarctic Bird	Mass
Adelie Penguin	6 kg 500 g
Emperor Penguin	45 kg
Cape Petrel	550 g
Giant Antarctic Petrel	5 kg
Snow Petrel	300 g

Measurement and Data 4-20

MD4-21 Pounds and Ounces

In the United States, the mass of small objects is also measured in **ounces.**
We write 1 **oz** for 1 ounce.

A slice of bread and a quarter of a small apple each weigh about 1 oz.

1. What is the mass of the group of objects?

   a) 2 slices of bread _____   b) 7 slices of bread _____

2. a) Five quarters (25¢ coins) weigh about 1 oz.

      What is the mass of 10 quarters? _____ 50 quarters? _____

   b) A quarter of a small apple weighs about 1 oz.

      How much does a whole apple weigh? _____

3. Estimate the mass of the object in ounces. Measure the mass to the nearest ounce.

   a) a small carton of juice   b) a banana

      Estimate: _____ Measure: _____   Estimate: _____ Measure: _____

   c) a shoe   d) a JUMP Math student book

      Estimate: _____ Measure: _____   Estimate: _____ Measure: _____

The mass of larger objects is also measured in **pounds.** We write 1 **lb** for 1 pound.

A small (1 pint) water bottle has a mass of about 1 lb.

1 pt

4. Circle the correct mass for the item.

   a)   b)   c)   d)

   13 oz or 13 lb   3 oz or 3 lb   80 oz or 80 lb $5\frac{1}{2}$ oz or $5\frac{1}{2}$ lb

5. Circle the unit that is more appropriate to measure the mass of the item.

   a) glass of milk   b) table   c) wolf   d) slice of cheese

   oz or lb   oz or lb   oz or lb   oz or lb

6. Estimate the mass of the object in pounds. Measure the mass to the nearest pound.

   a) a backpack   b) a large full water bottle

      Estimate: _____ Measure: _____   Estimate: _____ Measure: _____

MD4-22 Converting Pounds to Ounces

1 pound = 16 ounces	1 lb = 16 oz

1. a) Fill in the table.

lb	1	2	3	4	5	6	7	8
oz	16							

   b) To change a measurement from pounds (lb) to ounces (oz), what number do you
   have to multiply by? _____

2. Change the measurement to ounces.

   a) 5 lb = _____   b) 9 lb = _____   c) 10 lb = _____   d) 100 lb = _____

   e) 30 lb = _____   f) 25 lb = _____   g) 200 lb = _____   h) 1,000 lb = _____

3. Convert the measurement in pounds to ounces. Then circle the greater measurement.

   a) 25 oz   (2 lb)   b) 65 oz   4 lb   c) 75 oz   5 lb
              32 oz

   d) 33 oz   3 lb   e) 10 lb   150 oz   f) 20 lb   350 oz

   g) 100 oz 10 lb   h) 10 lb   200 oz   i) 100 lb   1,575 oz

4. Use the table in Question 1.

   a) Write a measurement in ounces that is between …

      i) 5 lb and 6 lb _____   ii) 7 lb and 8 lb _____

   b) Write a measurement in pounds that is between …

      i) 50 oz and 70 oz _____   ii) 100 oz and 120 oz _____

5. Linh weighs 104 oz at birth. Miguel weighs 7 lb at birth. Who is heavier? Explain.

6. A male beaver weighs 62 lb. A female beaver weighs 46 lb.

   a) How much heavier is the male beaver than the female?

   b) How much do the beavers weigh together?

MD4-23 Capacity

The **capacity** of a container is how much it can hold.

1. Circle the container with greater capacity in real life.

a)

b)

Capacity is measured in **liters** (L).

A quart and $\frac{1}{4}$ of a cup together make about 1 L.

---

2. Circle the objects that have capacity less than 1 L. Cross out the objects that have capacity more than 1 L.

   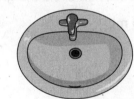   

3. a) Ronny says he drank 1 L of juice without stopping. Is that reasonable?

Explain. _____

b) Muriel says she needs 1 L of water to take a bath. Is that reasonable?

Explain. _____

Small quantities of liquid are measured in **milliliters (mL)**. One teaspoon holds 5 mL of liquid.

---

4. Circle the best unit to measure the capacity of the object.

a) a cup of tea

   mL   L

b) a raindrop

   mL   L

c) a bathtub

   mL   L

d) a medicine bottle

   mL   L

e) a bucket of ice cream

   mL   L

f) a large can of paint

   mL   L

5. Clare filled a measuring cup with 40 mL of water.
She poured out some water. There were 30 mL left.

How much water did she pour out?

1 liter = 1,000 milliliters	1 L = 1,000 mL

6. Fill in the table.

L	1	2	3	4	5	6	7	8
mL	1,000							

7. To change a measurement from liters (L) to milliliters (mL), what number do you multiply by? _____

8. Change the following measurements to milliliters.

a) 3 L = _____   b) 9 L = _____   c) 12 L = _____   d) 50 L = _____

9. Convert the measurement in liters to milliliters. Then circle the greater measurement.

a) 500 mL   ⬭3 L⬭   b) 5,300 mL   9 L   c) 24,567 mL   24 L
     3,000 mL

d) 4,444 mL   4 L   e) 80 L   8,600 mL   f) 72 L   55,203 mL

10. a) Write a measurement in milliliters that is between 5 L and 6 L. _____

b) Write a measurement in liters that is between 3,905 mL and 4,603 mL. _____

11. Convert the measurements in milliliters to mixed measurements.

a) 5,130 mL = ___5___ L ___130___ mL   b) 8,217 mL = _____ L _____ mL

c) 2,367 mL = _____ L _____ mL   d) 4,081 mL = _____ L _____ mL

e) 7,008 mL = _____ L _____ mL   f) 30,890 mL = _____ L _____ mL

12. Convert the mixed measurements to measurements in milliliters.

a) 3 L 8 mL = ___3,008___ mL   b) 4 L 510 mL = _____ mL

c) 4 L 545 mL = _____ mL   d) 5 L 402 mL = _____ mL

e) 6 L 7 mL = _____ mL   f) 17 L 57 mL = _____ mL

BONUS ▶ 123 L 456 mL = _____ mL

Measurement and Data 4-23

MD4-24 Problems with Capacity and Mass

1. Circle "true" or "false."

   a) You would measure the weight of a car in liters.   true   false

   b) A gram is used to measure volume.   true   false

   c) The contents of a can of soda are usually measured in kilograms.   true   false

   d) Grams are used to measure the mass of objects.   true   false

   e) Milliliters are used to measure capacity.   true   false

2. Write a unit of measurement to make each statement reasonable.

   a) A teacup holds about 200 _____ of tea.

   b) A chair has a mass of about 4 _____.

   c) An adult house cat weighs over 1,000 _____.

   d) A bucket holds about 8 _____ of water.

   e) A slice of bread weighs about 1 _____.

3. Aaron used a mug with a capacity of 250 mL to fill a pot with water. He filled and
   emptied the mug 4 times to fill the pot.

   What was the pot's capacity? _____

   Write the capacity using different units. _____

4. How many containers of the given capacity would be needed to make 1 liter?

   a) 250 mL _____   b) 100 mL _____   c) 200 mL _____   d) 500 mL _____

5. A cat weighs 5 kg. An airline will allow the cat on board if the cat and the cage weigh
   no more than 8 kg. What is the largest possible weight of the cage?

6. A café sold 1,500 cups of coffee, 250 mL each. How many liters of coffee did the café sell?

7. A pair of shoes in a box weighs $\frac{3}{4}$ lb. How much do 200 boxes of shoes weigh?

8. a) How many containers of size C would hold 20 L?

   b) How many containers of size A would hold as much water
      as 3 containers of size B?

   c) Which holds more: 4 containers of size B
      or 3 containers of size C?

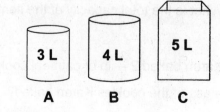

9. a) In the recipes below, circle the measurements of capacity and underline the measurements of mass.

  b) Total the measurements of mass in each recipe.

  c) Total the measurements of capacity in each recipe.

Ice Cream

1 kg fresh fruit

50 mL lemon juice

250 mL heavy cream

250 mL light cream

150 g sugar

Mass: _____

Capacity: _____

Tomato Sauce

30 mL olive oil

800 mL tomatoes

30 mL tomato paste

5 g fresh oregano

2 g fresh basil

Mass: _____

Capacity: _____

Birthday Cake

115 g butter

300 g sugar

3 eggs

280 g flour

5 g baking powder

150 mL milk

175 g chocolate

250 mL heavy cream

Mass: _____

Capacity: _____

Chana Masala

45 mL olive oil

6 oz onion

$\frac{1}{4}$ *oz garlic*

$2\frac{1}{4}$ *oz spices*

125 mL tomato paste

38 oz canned chickpeas

30 mL lemon juice

Mass: _____

Capacity: _____

10. Jenna is carrying groceries. In her bag there is a 1 L jug of milk, a 500 mL bottle of olive oil, a 500 mL bottle of vinegar, and a 700 mL jar of tomato sauce.

What is the total capacity of the items in milliliters?

What is the total capacity of the items as a mixed measurement?

11. Karen baked $2\frac{3}{4}$ lb of oatmeal cookies and $3\frac{1}{4}$ lb of raisin cookies. What is the total mass of the cookies Karen baked?

BONUS ▶ How many ounces of cookies did Karen bake?

OA4-39 Organized Lists

Find all the ways you can make 25¢ using dimes and nickels.

Step 1: List all the possible numbers of dimes in the solution in order: 0 dimes, 1 dime, 2 dimes (3 dimes would be too many).

Dimes	Nickels
0	
1	
2	

Step 2: Count by 5s to 25 to find out how many nickels you need to add to the dimes to make 25¢.

Dimes	Nickels
0	5
1	3
2	1

1. Fill in the number of pennies or nickels you need to make each amount.

a) 29¢

Dimes	Pennies
0	
1	
2	

b) 45¢

Dimes	Nickels
0	
1	
2	
3	
4	

c) 24¢

Nickels	Pennies
0	
1	
2	
3	
4	

d) 35¢

Dimes	Nickels
0	
1	
2	
3	

e) 80¢

Quarters	Nickels
0	
1	
2	
3	

f) 95¢

Quarters	Nickels
0	
1	
2	
3	

2. Kyle wants to find all the ways he can make 55¢ using quarters and nickels. He lists the number of quarters in increasing order. Why did he stop at 2 quarters?

_____

_____

Quarters	Nickels
0	
1	
2	

3. Fill in the number of pennies, nickels, dimes, or quarters you need to make each amount. Hint: You may not need to use all of the rows.

a) 13¢

Dimes	Pennies

b) 35¢

Dimes	Nickels

c) 80¢

Quarters	Nickels

4. Birds have 2 legs, cats have 4 legs, and ants have 6 legs. Complete the charts to find out how many legs each combination of 2 animals has in total.

a)

Birds	Cats	Total Number of Legs
0	2	
1	1	
2	0	

b)

Birds	Ants	Total Number of Legs
0	2	
1	1	
2	0	

5. Fill in the chart to find the solution to the problem.

a)

Birds	Dogs	Total Number of Legs

Two pets have a total of 6 legs
Each pet is either a bird or a dog.

How many of each are there?

b)

Birds	Cats	Total Number of Legs

Three pets have a total of 8 legs.
Each pet is either a bird or a cat.

How many of each are there?

OA4-40 Factors

You can make only three different rectangles out of 4 squares.

The numbers of squares across the rectangles are called the **factors** of 4.

The factors of 4 are 1, 2, and 4.

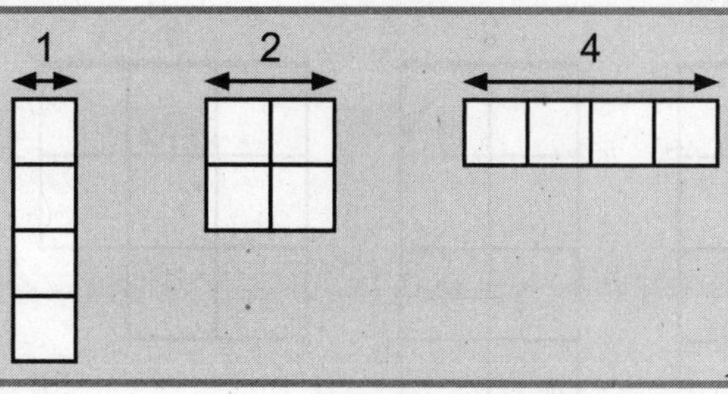

1. Finish drawing the rectangle so that it has 6 squares in total. The first one is done for you.

   a) 1 square across

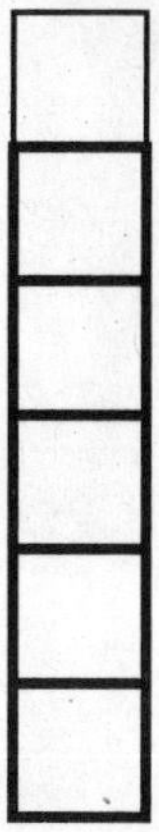

   b) 2 squares across

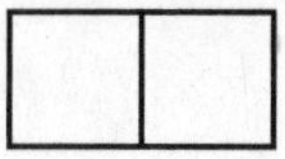

   c) 3 squares across

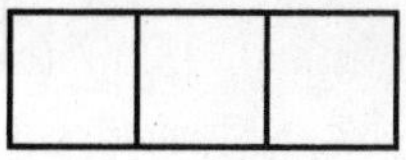

The rectangles you drew in Question 1 show that 1, 2, and 3 are factors of 6.

Jacob tries to make a rectangle with 4 squares across and 6 squares in total. He can't finish the rectangle.

Jacob's picture shows that 4 is not a factor of 6.

4 squares across

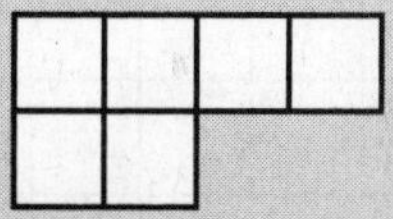

2. Use the picture to answer the question.

   a) Is 5 a factor of 6? _____

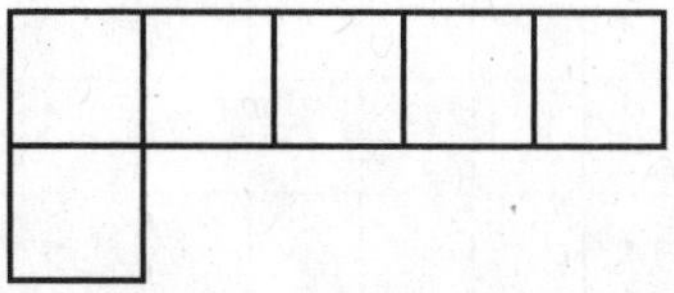

   b) Is 6 a factor of 6? _____

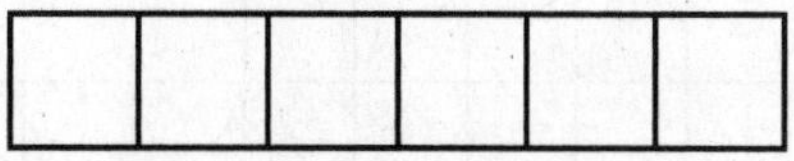

3. a) Can a rectangle with 7 squares across have only 6 squares altogether? _____

   Is 7 a factor of 6? _____

   b) Is 534 a factor of 6? How do you know? _____

   _____

4. Circle the rectangles. Then list the factors of 8.

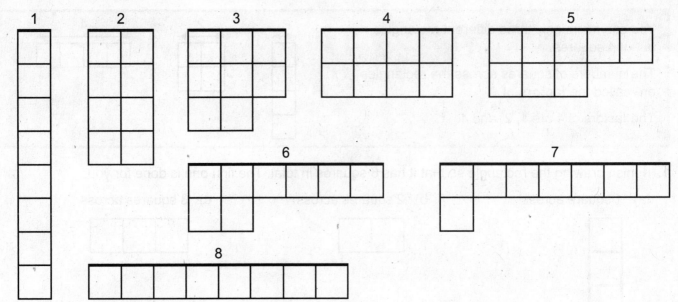

1   2   3   4   5   6   7

8

The factors of 8 are _____, _____, _____, and _____.

5. Draw the rectangles that show the factors of the number. Then list the factors below.

a) 9

b) 10

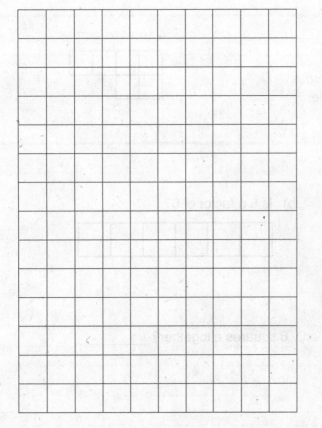

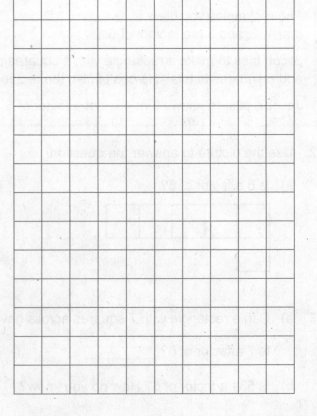

The factors of 9 are _____.

The factors of 10 are _____.

Operations and Algebraic Thinking 4-40

OA4-41 Finding Factors

You can check for factors of a number by skip counting.

Example 1: Is 2 a factor of 8? Draw rectangles with 2 squares across to check.

2   4·   6   8 ←——— yes, 2 **is** a factor of 8

Example 2: Is 5 a factor of 12? Draw rectangles with 5 squares across to check.

5   10   15 ←——— too far, so 5 **is not** a factor of 12

1. Is 3 a factor of 8? Draw rectangles to check.

Sara draws one rectangle to check if 4 is a factor of 18.
She makes one row, and then she keeps adding rows as
she skip counts by 4.

Sara passes 18 when skip counting, so 4 is not a factor of 18.

4
8
12
16
20

2. Is 5 a factor of 18? Use Sara's method to check.

3. Skip count to check for factors.   *Skip counting:*

   a) Is 3 a factor of 10? _____   _____, _____, _____, _____, _____

   b) Is 2 a factor of 8? _____   _____, _____, _____, _____, _____

   c) Is 20 a factor of 90? _____   _____, _____, _____, _____, _____

   d) Is 33 a factor of 99?   e) Is 51 a factor of 96?   f) Is 24 a factor of 72?

If **two** whole numbers multiply to make 12, they are called **factors** of 12.

Example: Skip counting shows that $12 = 4 \times 3$.
So 3 is a factor of 12.

4. **a)** Write what you multiply by to get 10. If there is no number, write **X**.

☐ × 1 = 10   ☐ × 6 = 10

☐ × 2 = 10   ☐ × 7 = 10

☐ × 3 = 10   ☐ × 8 = 10

☐ × 4 = 10   ☐ × 9 = 10

☐ × 5 = 10   ☐ × 10 = 10

b) The factors of 10 are _____, _____, _____, and _____.

REMINDER ▶ You can write a division with remainder 0 for every multiplication.
Example: $3 \times 4 = 12$, so $12 \div 3 = 4 \text{ R } 0$

5. Write a division with remainder 0 for the multiplication.

a) $3 \times 5 = 15$ so _____   **b)** $4 \times 6 = 24$ so _____

c) $2 \times 8 = 16$ so _____   **d)** $5 \times 6 = 30$ so _____

You can use division to check for factors.

Example: 3 is a factor of 12 because $12 \div 3$ has remainder 0.

6. **Use** division to check if 3 is a factor.

a) $11 \div 3 = $ _____ R _____   **b)** $18 \div 3 = $ _____ R _____

Is 3 a factor of 11? _____   Is 3 a factor of 18? _____

c) $21 \div 3 = $ _____ R _____   **d)** $16 \div 3 = $ _____ R _____

Is 3 a factor of 21? _____   Is 3 a factor of 16? _____

e) $14 \div 3 = $ _____ R _____   **f)** $27 \div 3 = $ _____ R _____

Is 3 a factor of 14? _____   Is 3 a factor of 27? _____

7. Use long division to check if 6 is a factor.

a) 96

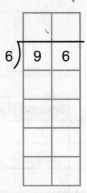

Is 6 a factor of 96? _____

b) 84

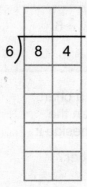

Is 6 a factor of 84? _____

c) 72

Is 6 a factor of 72? _____

d) 80

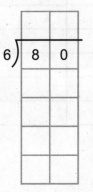

Is 6 a factor of 80? _____

e) 92

Is 6 a factor of 92? _____

f) 78

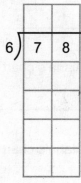

Is 6 a factor of 78? _____

8. Use long division to check for factors.

a) Is 7 is a factor of 84? _____

b) Is 4 a factor of 94? _____

c) Is 3 a factor of 87? _____

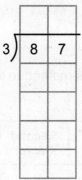

9. Would you use skip counting or long division to answer each question? Explain your choice.

a) Is 23 a factor of 92?

b) Is 3 a factor of 92?

OA4-42 Factor Pairs

> 2 and 3 are a **factor pair** of 6 because $2 \times 3 = 6$.
>
> 2 and 2 are a factor pair of 4 because $2 \times 2 = 4$.

1. Alana lists the factor pairs of 10 by making a chart. She tries all the numbers from 1 to 10. When the first number isn't a factor, she writes an ✗ beside it.

First Number	Second Number
1	10
2	5
3 ✗	
4 ✗	
5	2
6 ✗	
7 ✗	
8 ✗	
9 ✗	
10	1

   a) Why doesn't Alana try 11 as a first number?

   _____

   _____

   b) Use Alana's chart to write the factors of 10.

   _____, _____, _____, and _____

   c) Use Alana's chart to write the factor pairs of 10:

   _____, _____   _____, _____   _____, _____   _____, _____

> Connor uses Alana's method to find all the factor pairs of 10, but he leaves out the numbers that are not factors.
>
> | First Factor | Second Factor |
> |---|---|
> | 1 | 10 |
> | 2 | 5 |
> | 5 | 2 |
> | 10 | 1 |

2. Use Connor's method to list all the factor pairs of each number.

   a) 12

First Factor	Second Factor

   b) 20

First Factor	Second Factor

   c) 18

First Factor	Second Factor

In a factor pair, each number can be the first factor. Example: If 3 is a first factor paired with 4, then 4 is a first factor paired with 3: $3 \times 4 = 4 \times 3 = 12$.

3. Use the top half of the chart to finish the bottom half. Part a) is done for you.

a) 18

First Factor	Second Factor
1	18
2	9
3	6
6	3
9	2
18	1

b) 28

First Factor	Second Factor
1	28
2	14
4	7
7	

c) 44

First Factor	Second Factor
1	44
2	22
4	11
11	

To list all the factor pairs of a number, stop when you get a number that is already part of a pair.

4. Make a chart to find all the factor pairs. There might be more rows than you need.

a) 20

First Factor	Second Factor
1	20
2	10
4	5
5, stop	

b) 81

First Factor	Second Factor
1	81
3	27
9	9, stop

c) 28

First Factor	Second Factor

d) 42

First Factor	Second Factor

e) 99

First Factor	Second Factor

f) 100

First Factor	Second Factor

BONUS ▶ Make a chart to find all the factors of 72.

1. List the factors of each number.

Number	Factors
2	*1, 2*
3	*1, 3*
4	*1, 2, 4*
5	
6	
7	
8	
9	
10	

Number	Factors
11	
12	
13	
14	
15	
16	
17	
18	
19	

2. The numbers greater than 1 are divided into **prime numbers** and **composite numbers**.

Prime	Composite
2, 3, 5, 7, 11, 13, 17, 19	4, 6, 8, 9, 10, 12, 14, 15, 16, 18

a) Circle the prime numbers in Question 1.

b) How many factors does each prime number have? _____

A whole number is called **prime** if it has exactly two factors. A whole number is called **composite** if it has more than two factors.

3. How many factors does the number 1 have? _____

Is the number 1 prime, composite, or neither? _____

4. a) Circle the prime numbers.

1   22   13   45   75   16   72   81   17   19   99

b) Is it faster to show that a prime number is prime or that a composite number is composite? Explain.

_____

_____

Any whole number is a **multiple** of each of its factors.

Example: $2 \times 3 = 6$, so 6 is a multiple of 2 and 6 is a multiple of 3.

5. Write "multiple" or "factor."

　a)　10 is a _____ of 2 and 2 is a _____ of 10.

　b)　10 is a _____ of 20 and 20 is a _____ of 10.

6. Skip count to check for multiples.　　*Skip counting:*

　a)　Is 36 a multiple of 8? _____　　_____, _____, _____, _____, _____

　b)　Is 42 a multiple of 9? _____　　_____, _____, _____, _____, _____

　c)　Is 35 a multiple of 7? _____　　_____, _____, _____, _____, _____

　d)　Is 24 a multiple of 6? _____　　_____, _____, _____, _____, _____

7. Use long division to decide if each number is a multiple of 4.

　a)

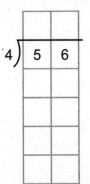

　　Is 56 a multiple of 4? _____

　b)

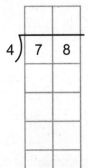

　　Is 78 a multiple of 4? _____

　c)

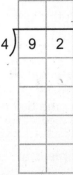

　　Is 92 a multiple of 4? _____

REMINDER ▶ An **even** number is a multiple of 2. So all even numbers have 2 as a factor.

8. a)　Finish writing the factor pair of the number.

　　i)　6　　　　ii)　20　　　　iii)　64　　　　**BONUS ▶** 48,426

　　　2 and _____　　2 and _____　　2 and _____　　　2 and _____

　b)　Which even numbers are composite? Explain. _____

　_____

　_____

OA4-44 Problem Solving with Factors (Advanced)

1. Circle the picture that shows the claim is not true.

a) All circles are shaded.

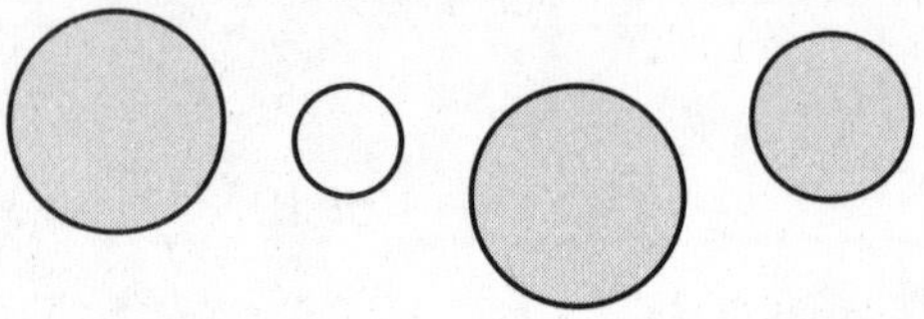

b) All squares are striped.

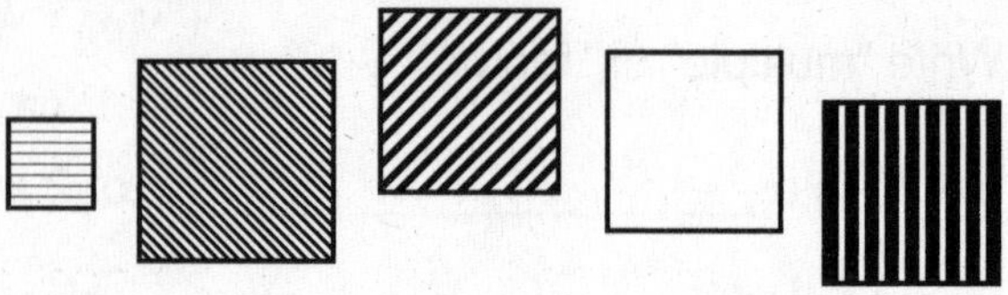

c) All triangles are white.

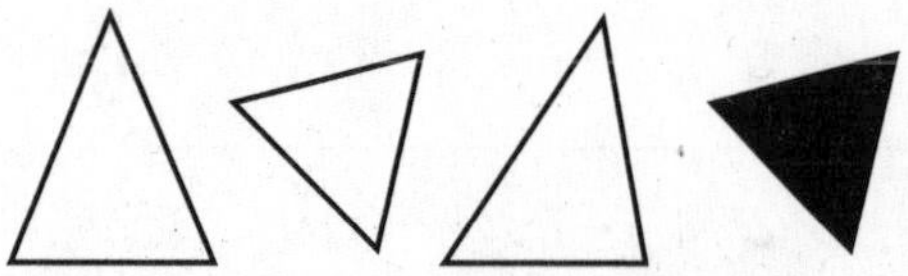

BONUS ▶ All shaded shapes are circles.

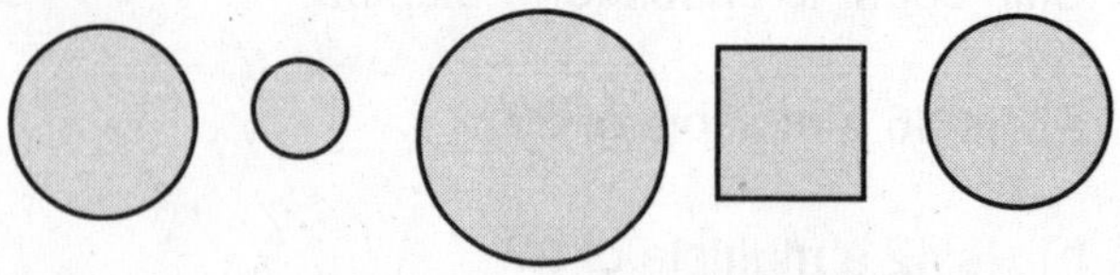

2. Which picture shows the claim is not true?

a) All triangles are shaded. _________

b) All triangles have a horizontal side. _________

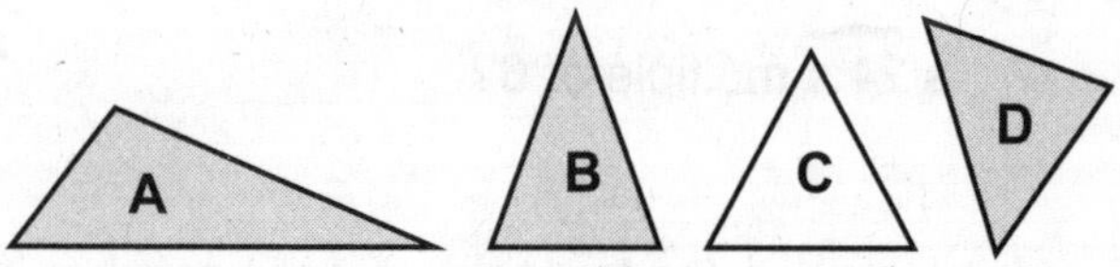

BONUS ▶ Which letter in the list shows the claim is not true?

A R U i E O

a) All letters are vowels. _________

b) All letters are capital letters. _________

c) All letters come before "t" in the alphabet. _________

A **counterexample** is an example that shows a statement is not true.

3. Circle the counterexample.

a) All words have a letter "b."

bed big buy globe stone

b) All names have five letters.

Jacob Mark Randy Darya

c) All prime numbers are odd.

2 3 5 7 11 13

d) All odd numbers are prime.

3 5 7 9 11 13

e) All composite numbers are even.

4 6 8 9 10 12

f) All even numbers are composite.

2 4 6 8 10 12

4. Put a check mark in front of the numbers that are composite numbers.

_____ 30 _____ 31 _____ 32 _____ 33 _____ 34 _____ 35 _____ 36 _____ 37

5. To show a claim is not true, you only need one example.
Circle the *first* example that shows the claim is not true.

a) All cars are white.

b) All girls are wearing glasses.

c) All numbers are even.

1   2   3   4   5   6   7   8   9   10   11   12

d) All numbers only have one digit.

1   2   3   4   5   6   7   8   9   10   11   12

e) All even numbers have ones digit 2.

2   4   6   8   10

f) All multiples of 3 have ones digit 3.

3   6   9   12   15

g) All numbers between 5 and 10 are even.

5   6   7   8   9   10

6. a) List the factors of 24. _____

How many odd factors does 24 have? _____

b) List the factors of 25. _____

How many even factors does 25 have? _____

7. I am a prime number less than 10. If you add 10 or 20 to me,
the result is a prime number. What number am I?

8. Find a counterexample to this statement: "The sum of two prime numbers is prime."

NF4-19 Dollar Notation and Cent Notation

The tables show how to represent money in cent notation and in dollar notation.

	Cent Notation	Dollar (Decimal) Notation
Sixty-five cents	65¢	$0.65

dimes   pennies

	Cent Notation	Dollar (Decimal) Notation
Seven cents	7¢	$0.07

dimes   pennies

The dot between the 0 and the number of dimes is called a **decimal point**.

1. Write the total amount of money in cent notation and in dollar (decimal) notation.

a)

Dimes	Pennies
3	4

= __34__ ¢ = $ __0.34__

b)

Dimes	Pennies
0	5

= _____ ¢ = $ _____

c)

Dimes	Pennies
4	3

= _____ ¢ = $ _____

d)

Dimes	Pennies
8	7

= _____ ¢ = $ _____

e)

Dimes	Pennies
5	4

= _____ ¢ = $ _____

f)

Dimes	Pennies
0	9

= _____ ¢ = $ _____

g)

Dimes	Pennies
0	2

= _____ ¢ = $ _____

h)

Dimes	Pennies
7	5

= _____ ¢ = $ _____

i)

Dimes	Pennies
0	1

= _____ ¢ = $ _____

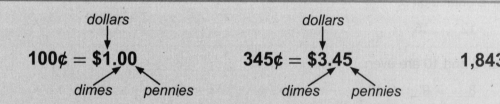

dollars   dollars   dollars

100¢ = $1.00   **345¢ = $3.45**   **1,843¢ = $18.43**

dimes   pennies   dimes   pennies   dimes   pennies

2. Complete the table. The first one is done for you.

	Amount in ¢	Dollars	Dimes	Pennies	Amount in $
a)	143¢	1	4	3	$1.43
b)	47¢				
c)	325¢				
d)	3¢				
e)	2,816¢				

Number and Operations—Fractions 4-19

3. Write each amount in cent notation.

a) $3.00 = _____   b) $0.60 = _____   c) $0.09 = _____   d) $1.00 = _____

e) $7.00 = _____   f) $12.00 = _____   g) $15.00 = _____   h) $1.99 = _____

i) $1.51 = _____   j) $0.98 = _____   k) $0.03 = _____   l) $0.08 = _____

4. Write each amount in dollar notation.

a) 254¢ = _$2.54_   b) 103¢ = _____   c) 216¢ = _____   d) 375¢ = _____

e) 300¢ = _____   f) 4¢ = _____   g) 7¢ = _____   h) 90¢ = _____

i) 600¢ = _____   j) 99¢ = _____   k) 1,200¢ = _____   l) 1,604¢ = _____

5. Complete the table as shown in part a).

	Dollars		Cents		Total
a)		= $3		= 35¢	$3.35
b)		= ___		= ___	___
c)		= ___		= ___	___
d)		= ___		= ___	___

6. Alicia paid for a pencil with 3 coins. The pencil cost $0.75. Which coins did she use?

7. Alan bought a pack of markers for $3.50. He paid for it with 5 pieces of money (bills and coins). Draw the money he used.

8. Show two ways to make $5.25 with 6 pieces of money (bills and coins).

NF4-20 More Dollar Notation and Cent Notation

> **REMINDER ▶** $1.00 = 100¢ $0.50 = 50¢ $0.05 = 5¢ $3.82 = 382¢

1. Change the amount in dollar notation to cent notation. Then circle the greater amount.

   a) (175¢) or $1.73   b) $1.00 or 101¢   c) 6¢ or $0.04
                  173¢

   d) $5.98 or 597¢   e) 650¢ or $6.05   f) $0.87 or 187¢

2. Write each amount in cent notation. Then circle the greater amount of money in the pair.

   a) three dollars and eighty-five cents   or   three dollars and twenty-eight cents

   _____   _____

   b) nine dollars and seventy cents   or   nine dollars and eighty-two cents

   _____   _____

   c) eight dollars and seventy-five cents   or $8.63

   _____   _____

   d) twelve dollars and sixty cents   or $12.06

   _____   _____

   e) eighty-nine cents   or   three dollars

   _____   _____

3. Write the amount in cent notation and then in dollar notation.

   a) 7 pennies = __7¢__ = __$0.07__ b) 4 nickels = _____ = _____   c) 6 dimes = _____ = _____

   d) 4 pennies = _____ = _____   e) 13 pennies = _____ = _____ f) 1 quarter = _____ = _____

   g) 5 nickels = _____ = _____   h) 3 quarters = _____ = _____ i) 8 dimes = _____ = _____

   j) 1 dollar = _____ = _____   k) 5 dollars = _____ = _____   l) 7 dollars = _____ = _____

4. Which is a greater amount of money: 168¢ or $1.65? Explain. _____

   _____

NF4-21 Tenths and Hundredths (Fractions)

A dime is $\frac{1}{10}$ of a dollar. A penny is $\frac{1}{100}$ of a dollar.

1. Write the fraction of a dollar the amount represents.

   a) 4 pennies ☐   b) 3 dimes ☐   c) 6 dimes ☐   d) 34 pennies

2. Write how many pennies the dimes are worth. Then write a fraction equation.

   a) 3 dimes = __30__ pennies

   $$\frac{3}{10} = \frac{30}{100}$$

   b) 7 dimes = _____ pennies

   c) 8 dimes = _____ pennies

   d) 5 dimes = _____ pennies

3. Complete the table. The first row is done for you.

	Fraction of a Dollar (Tenths)	Number of Dimes	Number of Pennies	Fraction of a Dollar (Hundredths)
a)	$\frac{4}{10}$	4	40	$\frac{40}{100}$
b)		6		
c)			90	
d)	$\frac{3}{10}$			

4. Sarah says 37 pennies are worth more than 5 dimes because 37 coins are more than 5 coins. Is she right? Explain.

5. Shade the same amount in the second square. Then count by 10s to write the number of hundredths.

   a)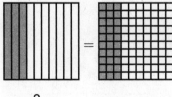

   $$\frac{3}{10} = \frac{}{100}$$

   b)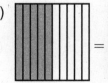

   $$\frac{5}{10} = \frac{}{100}$$

6. Count the columns to write the tenths. Count by 10s to write the hundredths.

a)

Picture	Tenths	Hundredths
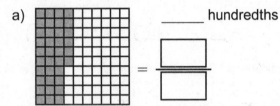	$\dfrac{2}{10}$	$\dfrac{20}{100}$

b)

Picture	Tenths	Hundredths
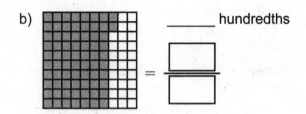		

7. Count the number of hundredths. Write your answer two ways.
Hint: Count by tens and then by ones.

a) 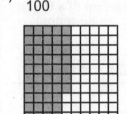 _____ hundredths

$= \dfrac{}{}$

b) 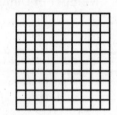 _____ hundredths

$= \dfrac{}{}$

8. Shade the fraction.

a) $\dfrac{47}{100}$ b) $\dfrac{3}{10}$ c) 5 hundredths   d) 4 tenths

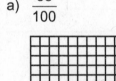

9. Shade the fraction. Then circle the greater fraction in each pair.

a) $\dfrac{38}{100}$ $\qquad$ $\dfrac{6}{10}$ $\qquad$ b) $\dfrac{4}{100}$ $\qquad$ $\dfrac{7}{10}$

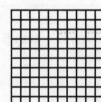

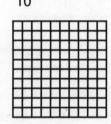

10. Rocco says that $\dfrac{17}{100}$ is greater than $\dfrac{8}{10}$ because 17 is greater than 8.

Is Rocco correct? Explain.

_____

_____

NF4-22 Decimal Tenths and Hundredths

A **tenth** (or $\frac{1}{10}$) can be represented in different ways.

A tenth of the distance between 0 and 1

A tenth of a pie

A tenth of a hundreds block

A tenth of a tens block

Tenths commonly appear in units of measurement ("a millimeter is a tenth of a centimeter").

Mathematicians invented decimal tenths as a short form for tenths: $\frac{1}{10} = 0.1$, $\frac{2}{10} = 0.2$, and so on.

1. Write a fraction and a decimal for each shaded part in the boxes below.

   a) $\dfrac{4}{10}$ 0.4

   b) $\dfrac{3}{10}$ 0.3

   c) $\dfrac{8}{10}$ 0.83

   d) $\dfrac{2}{10}$ 0.2

2. Write the decimal.

   a) 5 tenths = _0.5_   b) 7 tenths = 0.7 c) 6 tenths = 0.6 d) 9 tenths = 0.9

3. Shade to show the decimal.

   a) 0.3   b) 0.8   c) 0.5   d) 0.4

4. Show the decimal on the number line.

   a) 0.8 of the distance from 0 to 1

   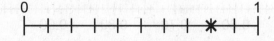

   b) 0.3 of the distance from 0 to 1

   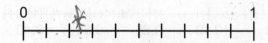

   c) 0.5 of the distance from 0 to 1

   d) 0.9 of the distance from 0 to 1

   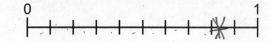

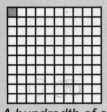

A **hundredth** (or $\frac{1}{100}$) can be represented in different ways:

0   1

A hundredth of a hundreds block

A hundredth of the distance from 0 to 1

Mathematicians invented decimal hundredths as a short form for hundredths.

Examples: $\frac{1}{100} = 0.01$, $\frac{8}{100} = 0.08$, $\frac{37}{100} = 0.37$

5. Write a fraction for the shaded part of the hundreds block. Then write the fraction as a decimal.
Hint: Count by 10s for each column or row that is shaded.

a) $\frac{60}{100} = 0.60$

b) $\frac{46}{100} = 0.46$

c) $\frac{18}{100} = 0.18$

d) $\frac{50}{100} = 0.5$

e) $\frac{47}{100} = 0.47$

BONUS ▶ 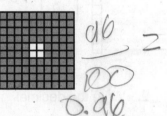 $\frac{96}{100} = 0.96$

6. Write the decimal hundredths.

a) 18 hundredths = _0.18_   b) 9 hundredths = _0.09_   c) 90 hundredths = _0.9_

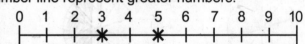

REMINDER ▶ Points farther to the right on a number line represent greater numbers.

Example: 5 is to the right of 3 because $5 > 3$.

0 1 2 3 4 5 6 7 8 9 10

7. a) Show the decimals on the number line.

A. 0.24   **B.** 0.70   **C.** 0.06   **D.** 0.45

b) Write the decimals in part a) from least to greatest.

_____ < _____ < _____ < _____

NF4-23 Comparing Decimal Tenths and Hundredths

1. Shade the same amount in the second square. Then count by 10s to find the number of hundredths. Write your answer as a fraction and a decimal.

a)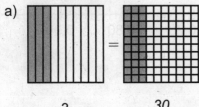

$$\frac{3}{10} = \frac{30}{100}$$

0.3 = _0.30_

b)

$$\frac{9}{10} = \frac{90}{100}$$

0.9 = _0.90_

c)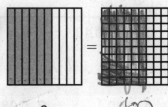

$$\frac{6}{10} = \frac{60}{100}$$

0.6 = _0.60_

2. a) Complete the table. The first row is done for you.

	Fraction Tenths	Fraction Hundredths	Picture	Decimal Tenths	Decimal Hundredths
i)	$\frac{2}{10}$	$\frac{20}{100}$		0.2	0.20
ii)	$\frac{7}{10}$	$\frac{70}{100}$		0.7	0.70
iii)	$\frac{4}{10}$	$\frac{40}{100}$		0.4	0.40

b) Use part a) to write the decimals from smallest to greatest: 0.40   0.2   0.7

$$0.2 < 0.7 < 0.40$$

3. Write how many tenths and how many hundredths. Then write an equation with decimals.

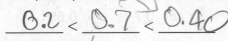

A. __20__ tenths
= __200__ hundredths
So __0.2__ = __0.2__

B. __10__ tenths
= __100__ hundredths
So __0.1__ = __1__

C. __20__ tenths
= __200__ hundredths
So __0.2__ = __2__

4. Show the decimals on the number line. Then write the decimals from least to greatest.

a) A. 0.40   B. 0.05   C. 0.27

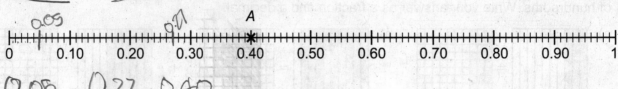

0.05 < 0.27 < 0.40

b) A. 0.80   B. 0.08   C. 0.05

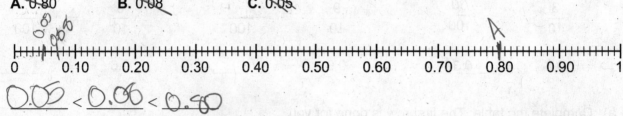

0.05 < 0.08 < 0.80

5. Write the decimal as a fraction with denominator 100.

a) $0.7 = \frac{7}{10} = \frac{70}{100}$ b) $0.48 = \frac{48}{100}$ c) $0.09 = \frac{9}{100}$ d) $0.3 = \frac{3}{100}$

6. Write the fraction as a decimal with 2 digits after the decimal point.

a) $\frac{6}{10} = 0.\underline{6}$
$= 0.\underline{6}\,\underline{0}$

b) $\frac{77}{100} = 0.\underline{7}\,\underline{7}$

c) $\frac{3}{10} = 0.\underline{3}$
$= 0.\underline{3}\,\underline{0}$

d) $\frac{9}{100} = 0.\underline{0}\,\underline{9}$

7. Circle the equalities that are incorrect.

$0.52 = \frac{52}{100}$ $0.8 = \frac{8}{10}$ $\frac{17}{100} = 0.17$ $\frac{3}{100} = 0.03$

$0.7 = \frac{7}{100}$ $0.53 = \frac{53}{100}$ $0.05 = \frac{5}{100}$ $0.02 = \frac{2}{10}$

8. Write the decimals as hundredths to compare the decimals. Then write < or >.

a) 0.4   0.73

$= \frac{4}{100}$ $= \frac{73}{100}$

0.4 $\boxed{<}$ 0.73

b) 0.2   0.16

$= \frac{2}{100}$ $= \frac{16}{100}$

0.2 $\boxed{<}$ 0.16

c) 0.7   0.59

$= \frac{7}{100}$ $= \frac{59}{100}$

0.7 $\boxed{<}$ 0.59

NF4-24 Combining Tenths and Hundredths

1. Describe the shaded fraction in four ways.

a)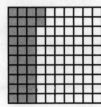

  _32_ hundredths = _3_ tenths _2_ hundredths

  $\frac{32}{100}$ = 0. _3_ _2_

b)

  ____ hundredths = ___ tenths ___ hundredths

  $\frac{}{100}$ = 0. ___ ___

c)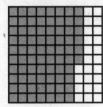

  ____ hundredths = ___ tenths ___ hundredths

  $\frac{}{100}$ = 0. ___ ___

d)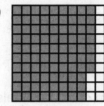

  ____ hundredths = ___ tenths ___ hundredths

  $\frac{}{100}$ = 0. ___ ___

2. Fill in the blanks.

a) 71 hundredths = _7_ tenths _1_ hundredth

  $\frac{71}{100}$ = 0. _7_ _1_

b) 28 hundredths = ____ tenths ____ hundredths

  $\frac{}{100}$ = 0. ___ ___

c) 41 hundredths = ____ tenths ____ hundredth

  $\frac{}{100}$ = 0. ___ ___

d) 60 hundredths = ____ tenths ____ hundredths

  $\frac{}{100}$ = 0. ___ ___

e) 8 hundredths = ____ tenths ____ hundredths

  $\frac{}{100}$ = 0. ___ ___

f) 2 hundredths = ____ tenths ____ hundredths

  $\frac{}{100}$ = 0. ___ ___

3. Describe each decimal in two ways.

a) 0.52 = _5_ tenths _2_ hundredths

  = _52 hundredths_

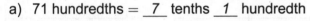

b) 0.83 = ____ tenths ____ hundredths

  = _____

c) 0.70 = ____ tenths ____ hundredths

  = _____

d) 0.02 = ____ tenths ____ hundredths

  = _____

Sohrab describes the distance covered on a number line in two ways.

43 hundredths = 4 tenths 3 hundredths

0.43

0   0.10   0.20   0.30   0.40   0.50   0.60   0.70   0.80   0.90   1

4. Write the distance covered in two ways.

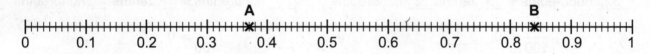

A

B

0   0.1   0.2   0.3   0.4   0.5   0.6   0.7   0.8   0.9   1

A. ____ tenths ____ hundredths

= ____ hundredths

B. ____ tenths ____ hundredths

= ____ hundredths

5. Estimate and mark the location of the decimals on the number line.

a) **A.** 0.62   **B.** 0.35   **C.** 0.99

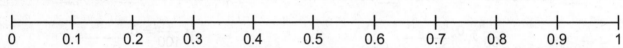

0   0.1   0.2   0.3   0.4   0.5   0.6   0.7   0.8   0.9   1

b) **A.** 0.37   **B.** 0.28   **C.** 0.51

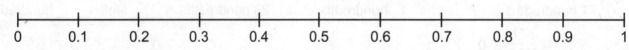

0   0.1   0.2   0.3   0.4   0.5   0.6   0.7   0.8   0.9   1

REMINDER ▶ A meter is 100 centimeters.

6. What part of a meter is the length shown? Write your answer as a decimal and a fraction.

a)

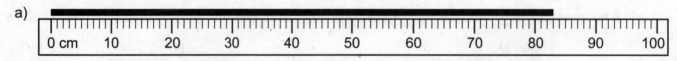

0 cm   10   20   30   40   50   60   70   80   90   100

83 cm = _0.83_ m = $\dfrac{83}{100}$ m

b)

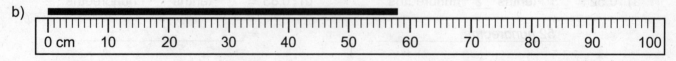

0 cm   10   20   30   40   50   60   70   80   90   100

58 cm = _____ m = [ ] m

NF4-25 Decimals and Money

A **dime** is **one tenth** of a dollar. A **penny** is **one hundredth** of a dollar.

1. Express the value of each decimal in four different ways.

a) 0.73

    7 dimes 3 pennies

    7 tenths 3 hundredths

    73 pennies

    73 hundredths

b) 0.62

c) 0.48

d) 0.03

e) 0.09

f) 0.19

2. Express the value of the decimal in four different ways.

a) 0.6 ____ dimes ____ pennies

    ____ tenths ____ hundredths

    ____ pennies

    ____ hundredths

b) 0.8 ____ dimes ____ pennies

    ____ tenths ____ hundredths

    ____ pennies

    ____ hundredths

3. Express the value of each decimal in four different ways. Then circle the greater number.

0.3 ____ dimes ____ pennies

    ____ tenths ____ hundredths

    ____ pennies

    ____ hundredths

0.18 ____ dimes ____ pennies

    ____ tenths ____ hundredths

    ____ pennies

    ____ hundredths

4. Will says 0.32 is greater than 0.5 because 32 is greater than 5. Can you explain his mistake?

1. Write the fraction addition for each statement.
   Hint: Replace "is the same amount of money as" with the equal sign (=).

   a) 1 dime and 2 pennies is the same amount of money as 12 pennies.

   $$\frac{1}{10} + \frac{2}{100} = \frac{12}{100}$$

   b) 3 dimes and 4 pennies is the same amount of money as 34 pennies.

   c) 2 dimes and 5 pennies is the same amount of money as _____ pennies.

2. Shade the total. Then write a fraction addition. Hint: Count by 10s for the columns you shaded.

   a)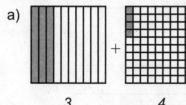

   $$\frac{3}{10} + \frac{4}{100} = \frac{34}{100}$$

   b)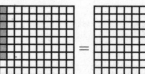

   c)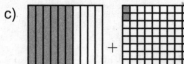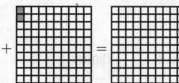

   d)

3. Shade the total. Then write a decimal addition.

   a)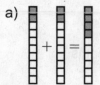

   b)

   c)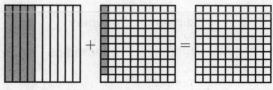

   $$0.2 + 0.2 = 0.4$$ _____   _____

To add $\dfrac{3}{10} + \dfrac{4}{100}$:

Step 1: Change the tenths to hundredths. $\dfrac{3 \times 10}{10 \times 10} = \dfrac{30}{100}$

Step 2: Add the hundredths. $\dfrac{30}{100} + \dfrac{4}{100} = \dfrac{34}{100}$

4. Write an equivalent fraction with denominator 100.

  a) $\dfrac{8}{10} = \dfrac{}{100}$

  b) $\dfrac{7}{10} = \dfrac{}{100}$

  c) $\dfrac{4}{10} =$

  d) $\dfrac{3}{10} =$

5. Add the hundredths.

  a) $\dfrac{20}{100} + \dfrac{3}{100}$

  b) $\dfrac{40}{100} + \dfrac{5}{100}$

  c) $\dfrac{70}{100} + \dfrac{2}{100}$

  d) $\dfrac{60}{100} + \dfrac{8}{100}$

  $= \dfrac{}{100}$

  $=$

  $=$

  $=$

6. Add the tenths and hundredths.

  a) $\dfrac{5}{10} + \dfrac{3}{100}$

  b) $\dfrac{3}{10} + \dfrac{7}{100}$

  c) $\dfrac{9}{10} + \dfrac{2}{100}$

  BONUS ▶ $\dfrac{7}{10} + \dfrac{15}{100}$

  $= \dfrac{}{100} + \dfrac{}{100}$

  $= \dfrac{}{100} + \dfrac{}{100}$

  $=$

  $=$

  $= \dfrac{}{100}$

  $= \dfrac{}{100}$

  $=$

  $=$

7. Add mentally.

  a) $\dfrac{7}{10} + \dfrac{4}{100} = \dfrac{}{100}$

  b) $\dfrac{6}{10} + \dfrac{9}{100} =$

  c) $\dfrac{1}{10} + \dfrac{9}{100} =$

  BONUS ▶ $\dfrac{8}{10} + \dfrac{13}{100} =$

8. Tyrell has $\dfrac{4}{10}$ of a dollar and Tania has $\dfrac{7}{100}$ of a dollar. What fraction of a dollar do they have altogether?

9. A snail crawled $\dfrac{3}{10}$ of a meter, and then crawled another $\dfrac{9}{100}$ of a meter. What fraction of a meter did the snail crawl altogether?

BONUS ▶ Abdi biked $\dfrac{7}{10}$ km on Monday and $\dfrac{29}{100}$ km on Tuesday. Did he bike more than a kilometer?

A mixed number can be written as a decimal.

Examples: $12\frac{3}{10} = 12.3$ $2\frac{85}{100} = 2.85$

The decimal point separates the whole number part (on the left) and the fraction part (on the right).

1. Write the mixed number as a decimal.

a) $3\frac{4}{10} =$ _____   b) $12\frac{5}{10} =$ _____   c) $8\frac{45}{100} =$ _____   d) $46\frac{3}{100} =$ _____

REMINDER ▶

The number of digits to the right of the decimal point = the number of zeros in the denominator

Examples: $3.\mathbf{45} = 3\frac{45}{\mathbf{100}}$ $34.5 = 34\frac{5}{10}$ $34.\mathbf{05} = 34\frac{5}{\mathbf{100}}$

2. Write the denominator of the fraction part for the equivalent mixed number.

a) 4.9 _____   b) 1.58 _____   c) 15.08 _____   **BONUS ▶** 18.3402 _____

3. Write the decimal as a mixed number.

a) 3.81 =   b) 6.9 =   c) 7.04 =   d) 18.15 =

e) 13.4 =   f) 17.06 =   g) 193.45 =   **BONUS ▶** 7.004 =

You can write a decimal in words. Use "and" for the decimal point.

Examples: $12\frac{3}{10} = 12.3 =$ twelve **and** three tenths $2\frac{85}{100} = 2.85 =$ two **and** eighty-five hundredths

4. Write "tenths" or "hundredths." Hint: Count the digits to the right of the decimal point.

a) 3.12 = three and twelve _____   b) 18.7 = eighteen and seven _____

c) 6.05 = six and five _____   d) 20.8 = twenty and eight _____

5. Write the equivalent words or decimal.

a) 7.4 = _____

b) 4.09 = _____

c) seventy-four and eleven hundredths = _____   d) twenty and four tenths = _____

> **REMINDER** ▶ You can change an improper fraction to a mixed number by dividing.
>
> Example: $\dfrac{28}{10}$
>
> $28 \div 10 = 2 \text{ R } 8$, so $\dfrac{28}{10} = 2\dfrac{8}{10}$

6. Change the improper fraction to a mixed number.

a) $\dfrac{74}{10}$ $74 \div 10 = $ _____ R _____

So $\dfrac{74}{10} = $

b) $\dfrac{684}{100}$ $684 \div 100 = $ _____ R _____

So $\dfrac{684}{100} = $

7. Change the improper fraction to a mixed number and then to a decimal.

a) $\dfrac{35}{10} = 3\dfrac{5}{10} = 3.5$

b) $\dfrac{387}{100} = 3\dfrac{87}{100} = 3.87$

c) $\dfrac{41}{10} = $

d) $\dfrac{642}{10} = $

e) $\dfrac{564}{100} = $

f) $\dfrac{4,208}{100} = $

8. Write the decimal as an improper fraction with denominator 10 or 100.

a) $3.8 = $

b) $7.08 = $

c) $8.60 = $

d) $60.04 = $

e) $70.8 = $

f) $17.5 = $

g) $31.89 = $

h) $90.4 = $

> Remember: $\dfrac{8}{10} = \dfrac{80}{100}$ So $2\dfrac{8}{10} = 2\dfrac{80}{100}$ So $2.8 = 2.80$

9. Complete the tables. Part a) is done for you.

	Decimal Tenths	Fraction Tenths	Fraction Hundredths	Decimal Hundredths
a)	2.7	$\dfrac{27}{10}$	$\dfrac{270}{100}$	2.70
b)	3.8			
c)	3.9			
d)	6.4			

	Decimal Tenths	Fraction Tenths	Fraction Hundredths	Decimal Hundredths
e)	59.4			
f)		$\dfrac{75}{10}$		
g)			$\dfrac{670}{100}$	
h)				30.80

Number and Operations—Fractions 4-27

121

NF4-28 Different Wholes (Advanced)

1. Write the fraction and the decimal.

   a) What fraction of a dime is a penny?

   A penny is worth _____ dimes.

   b) What fraction of a dollar is a penny?

   A penny is worth _____ dollars.

2. a) Hiro has pennies worth 0.5 dimes. How many pennies does he have? _____

   b) Naomi has pennies worth 0.5 dollars. How many pennies does she have? _____

   c) Who has more pennies? _____

3. a) Adam has pennies worth 0.4 dimes. How many pennies does he have? _____

   b) Rashida has pennies worth 0.25 dollars. How many pennies does she have? _____

   c) Who has more pennies? _____

   d) Rashida thinks 0.25 is more than 0.4 because she has more money.
      Is she correct? Explain.

   _____

   _____

4. Sarah says 0.25 is more than 0.3 because more is shaded. Is she right? Explain.

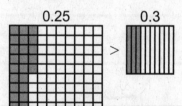

0.25   >   0.3

   _____

   _____

   _____

5. Is it possible for 0.3 of one square to be more than 0.4 of another square?
   Show your thinking with a picture.

6. Is it possible for 0.3 on one number line to be farther right than 0.5 on another number line?
   Show your thinking with a picture.

NF4-29 Problems and Puzzles

1. Add and then write the equation in decimal form.

   a) $3 + \frac{24}{100} = 3\frac{24}{100}$ b) $2 + \frac{8}{10} =$ c) $5 + \frac{7}{100} =$ d) $9 + \frac{53}{100} =$

   $3 + 0.24 = 3.24$

2. Write how many tenths are in each number. Then add and subtract.

   $2.3 = \rule{1.5cm}{0.15mm}$ tenths and $1.4 = \rule{1.5cm}{0.15mm}$ tenths.   So $2.3 + 1.4$ $2.3 - 1.4$

   $= \rule{1cm}{0.15mm}$ tenths $= \rule{1cm}{0.15mm}$ tenths

   $= \dfrac{\rule{1cm}{0.15mm}}{10}$ $= \dfrac{\rule{1cm}{0.15mm}}{10}$

   $= \rule{1cm}{0.15mm} . \rule{1cm}{0.15mm}$ $= \rule{1cm}{0.15mm} . \rule{1cm}{0.15mm}$

3. a) Write three decimal hundredths between 0.3 and 0.4. $\rule{1.5cm}{0.15mm}$, $\rule{1.5cm}{0.15mm}$, $\rule{1.5cm}{0.15mm}$

   b) Add 5 to your answers to part a). $\rule{1.5cm}{0.15mm}$, $\rule{1.5cm}{0.15mm}$, $\rule{1.5cm}{0.15mm}$
      Hint: Use the pattern you observed in your answers to Question 1.

   c) Your answers to part b) are between what two tenths? $\rule{1.5cm}{0.15mm}$ and $\rule{1.5cm}{0.15mm}$

4. a) How many cents are in 3 dollars? <u>300</u>

      How many cents are in 3 dollars and 8 cents? <u>308</u>

   b) How many centimeters are in 3 meters? $\rule{2cm}{0.15mm}$

      How many centimeters are in 3 meters and 8 centimeters? $\rule{2cm}{0.15mm}$

   c) How many ounces are in 3 pounds? $\rule{2cm}{0.15mm}$

      How many ounces are in 3 pounds and 8 ounces? $\rule{2cm}{0.15mm}$

   d) What is more like cents: centimeters or ounces? Explain.

5. Gia biked 2 km to school, $\frac{8}{10}$ km to the library, and then $2\frac{9}{100}$ km home. How far did Gia bike altogether?

6. Miguel has red, blue, and yellow marbles. $\frac{7}{10}$ are red and $\frac{6}{100}$ are blue. What fraction is yellow?

MD4-25 Inches

An **inch** (in) is a unit of measurement for **length** (or **height** or **thickness**). Inches are used in the United States.

Two fingers are about one inch wide.

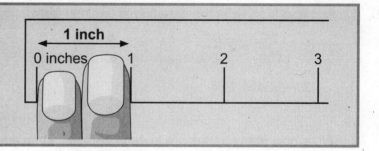

1. Measure a pencil and a shoe using two fingers.

   a) My pencil is about _____ inches long.   b) My shoe is about _____ inches long.

2. Select two objects in the classroom to measure with your fingers.

   a) _____ is about _____ inches long.

   b) _____ is about _____ inches long.

You can count hops to measure in inches the same way you do to measure in centimeters.

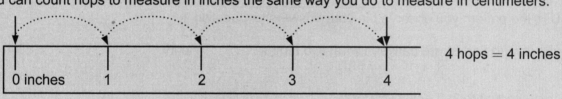

4 hops = 4 inches

3. Measure the distance between the arrows.

   a)
   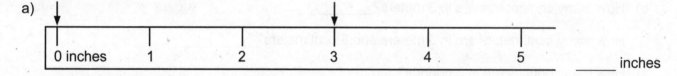
   _____ inches

   b)
   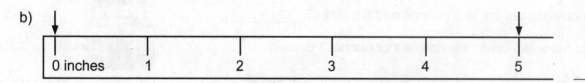
   _____ inches

   c)
   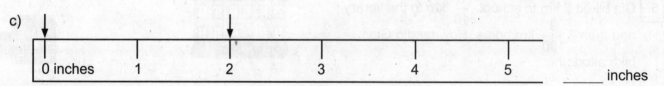
   _____ inches

   BONUS ▶
   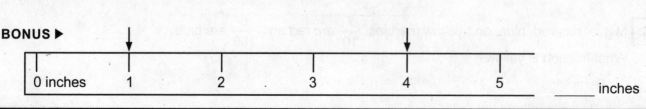
   _____ inches

4. Measure the length of each line segment or object.

a)

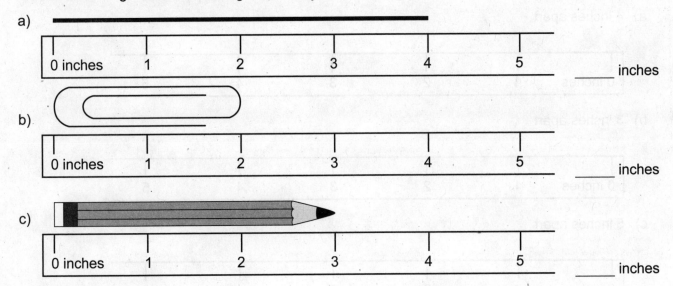

0 inches   1   2   3   4   5   _____ inches

b)

0 inches   1   2   3   4   5   _____ inches

c)

0 inches   1   2   3   4   5   _____ inches

5. a) Measure all the sides of each shape.

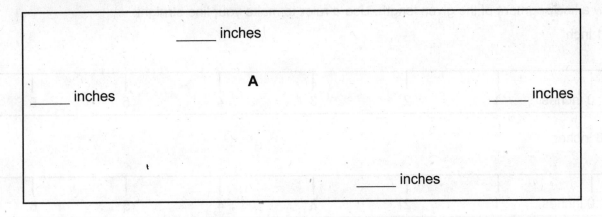

_____ inches

A

_____ inches   _____ inches

_____ inches

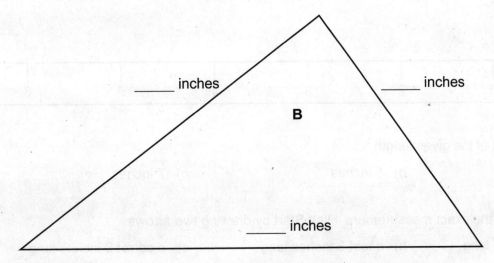

_____ inches   _____ inches

B

_____ inches

b) The **perimeter** is the distance around a shape. Find the perimeter of each shape in part a).

Perimeter of A = _____   Perimeter of B = _____

Measurement and Data 4-25

6. On each ruler, draw two arrows for the given distance. Start at the "0" mark.

a) 4 inches apart

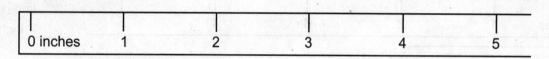

b) 3 inches apart

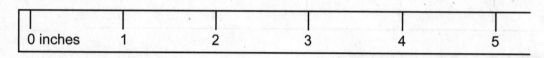

c) 5 inches apart

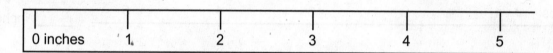

7. Draw a line segment of the given length. Use a ruler to make your line straight.

a) 1 inch

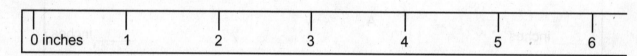

b) 6 inches

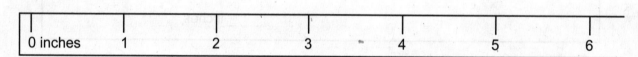

c) 2 inches

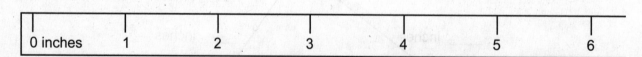

8. Draw a line segment of the given length.

a) 2 inches   b) 5 inches   c) 7 inches

9. Draw each object to the exact measurement. Hint: Start by drawing two arrows.

a) a pencil 4 inches long   b) a leaf 3 inches long   c) a carrot 6 inches long

10. On grid paper, draw a rectangle with a length of 3 inches and a width of 2 inches.

Measurement and Data 4-25

MD4-26 Quarters of an Inch

On some rulers, an inch is divided into 4 equal parts, but the mixed numbers are not written.

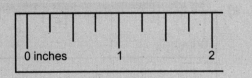

1. Write the missing mixed numbers. Use the smallest denominator you can.

a)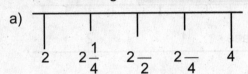

$2 \qquad 2\frac{1}{4} \qquad 2\frac{}{2} \qquad 2\frac{}{4} \qquad 4$

b)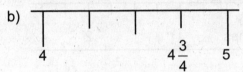

$4 \qquad\qquad\qquad 4\frac{3}{4} \qquad 5$

c)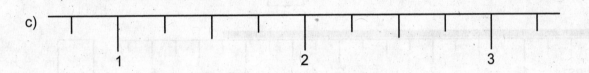

$\qquad 1 \qquad\qquad 2 \qquad\qquad 3$

2. Circle the mark for the mixed number or fraction.

a) $3\frac{1}{4}$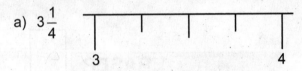

$3 \qquad\qquad 4$

b) $5\frac{3}{4}$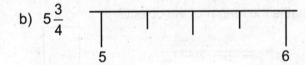

$5 \qquad\qquad 6$

c) $2\frac{3}{4}$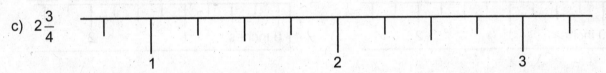

$1 \qquad\qquad 2 \qquad\qquad 3$

d) $\frac{1}{4}$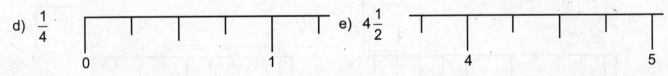

$0 \qquad\qquad 1$

e) $4\frac{1}{2}$

$4 \qquad\qquad 5$

f) $2\frac{1}{4}$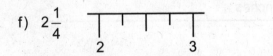

$2 \qquad 3$

g) $\frac{3}{4}$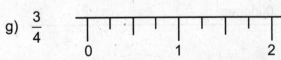

$0 \qquad 1 \qquad 2$

h) $7\frac{1}{2}$

$7 \qquad 8 \qquad 9$

i) $10\frac{1}{4}$

$9 \qquad 10 \qquad 11$

BONUS ▶ Mark the letter for each number on the number line. **A.** $2\frac{3}{4}$ **C.** $4\frac{1}{4}$ **E.** $5\frac{1}{2}$ **R.** $\frac{1}{2}$

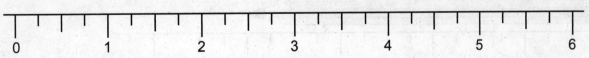

$0 \qquad 1 \qquad 2 \qquad 3 \qquad 4 \qquad 5 \qquad 6$

What word do you get if you write the letters in order? _____ _____ _____ _____

3. How long is the bar?

a)
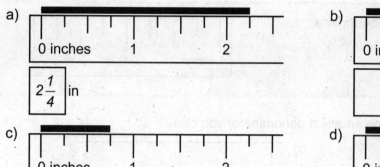

$2\dfrac{1}{4}$ in

b)
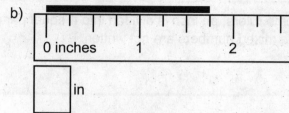

☐ in

c)
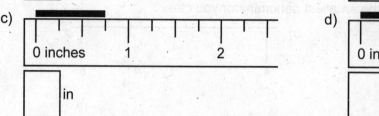

☐ in

d)
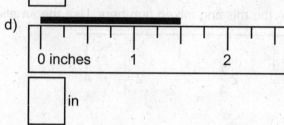

☐ in

e)
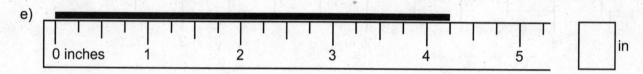

☐ in

4. What is the length of the object?

a)
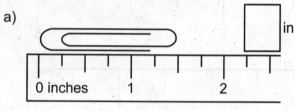

☐ in

b)
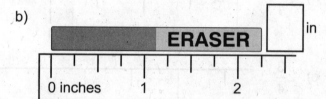

☐ in

c)
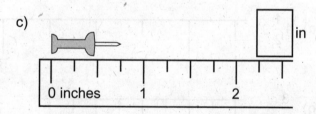

☐ in

d)
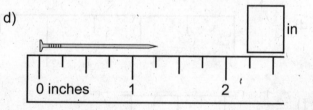

☐ in

e)
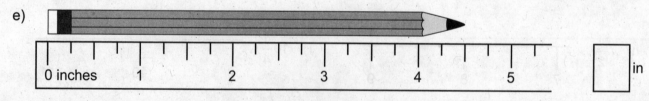

☐ in

BONUS ▶ Is this pencil exactly 4 inches long? How do you know?

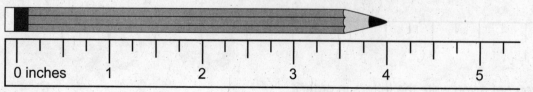

128

This rectangle is about $1\frac{1}{4}$ inch long.

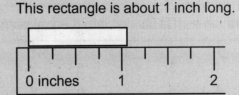

It is $1\frac{1}{4}$ inch long to the nearest quarter of an inch.

This rectangle is about 1 inch long.

It is 1 inch long to the nearest quarter of an inch.

5. What is the length of the bar to the nearest quarter of an inch?

a)
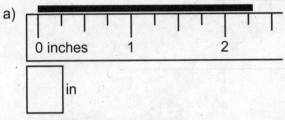

[ ] in

b)
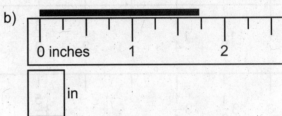

[ ] in

c)
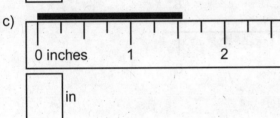

[ ] in

d)
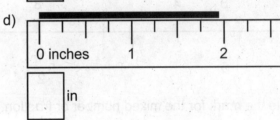

[ ] in

6. Measure the line segment to the nearest quarter of an inch.

a)

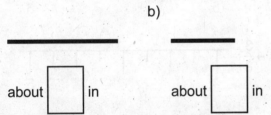

about [ ] in

b)

about [ ] in

c)

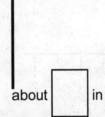

about [ ] in

d)

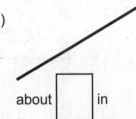

about [ ] in

7. Measure the sides of the rectangle and the dashed line to the nearest quarter of an inch.

a) about [ ] in

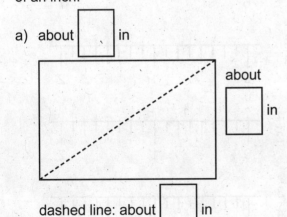

about [ ] in

dashed line: about [ ] in

b) about [ ] in

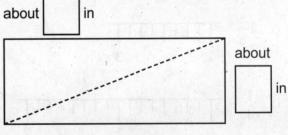

about [ ] in

dashed line: about [ ] in

BONUS ▶ Find the perimeter of the rectangles in Question 7. Which perimeter is larger?

MD4-27 Eighths of an Inch

On some rulers, an inch is divided into 8 equal parts. This ruler is enlarged to show the fractions.

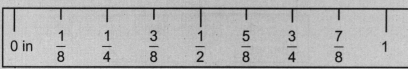

1. Write the missing mixed numbers on the number line.

a)

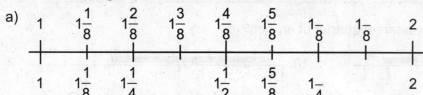

b)

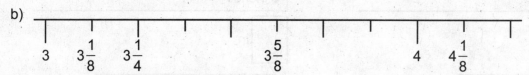

c)

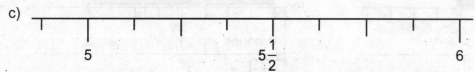

2. Circle the mark for the mixed number or fraction.

a) $3\frac{1}{8}$
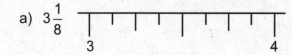

b) $5\frac{5}{8}$

c) $1\frac{3}{4}$
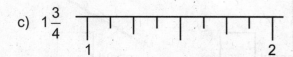

d) $4\frac{3}{8}$

e) $2\frac{1}{2}$
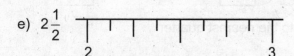

f) $6\frac{7}{8}$

g) $2\frac{3}{8}$
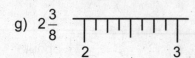

h) $\frac{5}{8}$

i) $\frac{1}{4}$
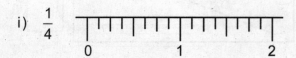

j) $1\frac{1}{2}$

k) $9\frac{7}{8}$
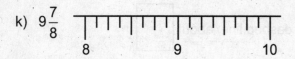

l) $9\frac{3}{4}$

Measurement and Data 4-27

3. How long is the bar or object?

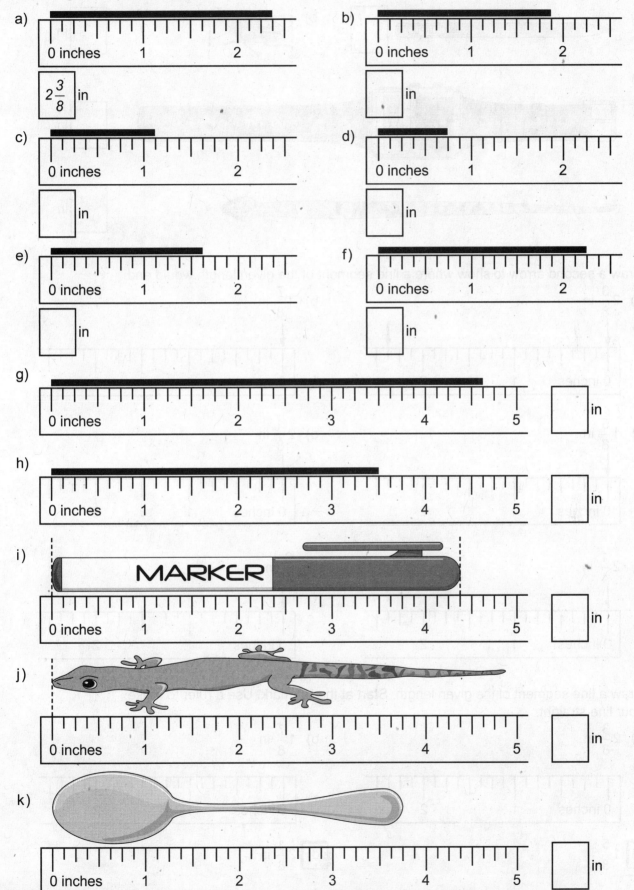

a) $2\frac{3}{8}$ in

b) ___ in

c) ___ in

d) ___ in

e) ___ in

f) ___ in

g) ___ in

h) ___ in

i) MARKER ___ in

j) ___ in

k) ___ in

4. Measure the object.

a)  in

b)  in

c)  in

d) in

5. Draw a second arrow to show where a line segment of the given length would end.

a) $2\frac{3}{8}$ in

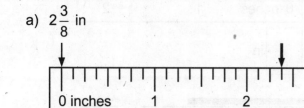

b) $1\frac{7}{8}$ in

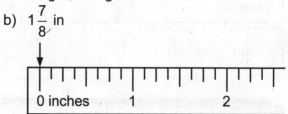

c) $1\frac{5}{8}$ in

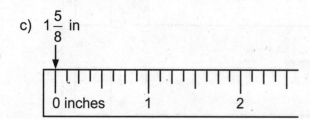

d) $2\frac{1}{8}$ in

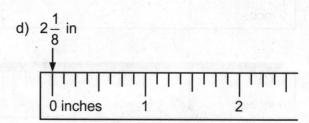

e) $2\frac{1}{4}$ in

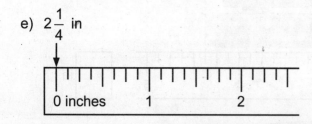

f) $\frac{3}{4}$ in

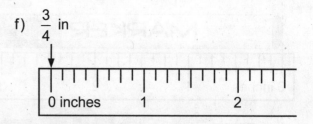

6. Draw a line segment of the given length. Start at the "0" mark. Use a ruler to make your line straight.

a) $2\frac{3}{8}$ in

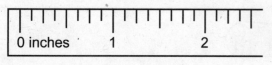

b) $1\frac{7}{8}$ in

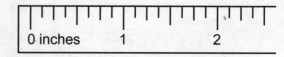

c) $1\frac{5}{8}$ in

d) $2\frac{1}{8}$ in

7. a) Draw a line segment with a length between ...

    i)   3 inches and 4 inches

    ii) $4\frac{1}{2}$ inches and 5 inches

    iii) $5\frac{1}{2}$ inches and $5\frac{3}{4}$ inches

    b) Measure each line segment you drew in part a) to the closest eighth of an inch.

    i) _____   ii) _____   iii) _____

8. Two pennies together are about $\frac{1}{8}$ inch thick.
    a) Find the height of each stack of pennies in eighths of an inch.

    i)   4 pennies _____   ii) 6 pennies _____   iii) 8 pennies _____

    b) Write each height as a fraction with the smallest denominator possible.

    i)   4 pennies _____   ii) 6 pennies _____   iii) 8 pennies _____

    c) How many pennies are in a stack 1 inch high? _____

9. Name an object that is about the given length. Then measure it to the nearest eighth of an inch.

    a) 1 inch _____   Length: _____

    b) 5 inches _____   Length: _____

    c) 12 inches _____   Length: _____

10. Use a ruler to draw the following objects to the exact length.

    a) Draw a line $4\frac{3}{4}$ inches long.   b) Draw a line $5\frac{5}{8}$ inches long.

    c) Draw a pencil $3\frac{1}{2}$ inches long.   d) Draw a flower 6 inches tall.

MD4-28 Feet

A **foot** (ft) is another unit of measurement for **length** (or **height** or **thickness**). Feet are used in the United States.

Your arm from knuckles to elbow is about 1 foot long.

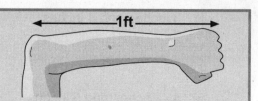
1ft

1. Circle the objects that are more than 1 foot long. Cross out the objects that are less than 1 inch long.

2. Measure the objects to the nearest foot using your arm.

   a) My desk is about _____ ft long.   b) A door is about _____ ft wide.

3. Select two objects in the classroom to measure with your arm.

   a) _____ is about _____ ft long.

   b) _____ is about _____ ft long.

4. Circle the unit that is more appropriate to measure the length of the item.

   a)   b)    c)    d)

   inch   foot   inch   foot   inch   foot   inch   foot

5. Circle the unit that is more appropriate to measure the height of the item.

   a)    b)    c)    d)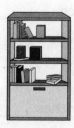

   inch   inch   inch   inch

   foot   foot   foot   foot

6. Estimate the distance to the nearest foot. Use a yardstick or a measuring tape to check your estimate in part a) or b).

   a) The length of a chalkboard is about _____ ft.

   b) The distance from the floor to the door handle is about _____ ft.

   I measured the distance in part _____. It is about _____ ft.

MD4-29 Feet and Inches

There are 12 inches in 1 foot.
1 ft = 12 in   2 ft = 24 in
The ruler is not to scale.

1	2	3	4	5	6	7	8	9	10	11	12	13	14	15	16	17	18	19	20	21	22	23	24
inches
feet   1 F   2 F

1. Fill in the measurements in inches.

feet	1	2	3	4	5	6	7	8
inches	12							

2. To change a measurement from feet (ft) to inches (in), what number do you

   have to multiply by? _____

3. Fill in the measurements in inches.

a)

ft	in
9	
10	
11	

b)

ft	in
20	
25	
30	

c)

ft	in
50	
100	
120	

4. Convert the measurement in feet to inches. Then circle the greater measurement.

a) 50 in   (7 ft)   b) 83 in   6 ft   c) 45 in   5 ft
              84 in

d) 111 in   11 ft   e) 10 ft   100 in   f) 20 ft   2,000 in

g) 30 ft   1,500 in   h) 555 in   50 ft   i) 100 ft   1,212 in

5. Write a measurement in inches that is between …

a) 6 ft and 7 ft _____   b) 7 ft and 8 ft _____   c) 11 ft and 12 ft _____

6. Write a measurement in feet that is between …

a) 67 in and 75 in _____   b) 27 in and 39 in _____   c) 100 in and 110 in _____

MD4-30 Measuring in Feet and Inches

Angie measures a box.

First she counts by feet, then by inches.

The box is 1 foot 3 inches long.

The ruler is not drawn to scale.

1. What is the length of the bar? Count by feet first, and then count by inches.

   a) _____ ft _____ in

   b) _____ ft _____ in

   c) _____ ft _____ in

2. a) Estimate each distance. Use your arm for feet and two fingers for inches.

   i)   Length of a desk: about _____ ft _____ in

   ii) Height of a desk: about _____ ft _____ in

   iii) Height of a chair: about _____ ft _____ in

   iv) Length of a meter stick: about _____ ft _____ in

   b) Measure each distance with a yardstick or a measuring tape.

   i)   Length of a desk: _____ ft _____ in

   ii) Height of a desk: _____ ft _____ in

   iii) Height of a chair: _____ ft _____ in

   iv) Length of a meter stick: _____ ft _____ in

3. Select two objects to estimate and measure in feet and inches.

   _____   _____

   Estimate: about _____ ft _____ in   Estimate: about _____ ft _____ in

   Actual: _____ ft _____ in   Actual: _____ ft _____ in

4.

   a) How long is the snake in feet? _____

   b) How long is the snake in inches? _____ How do you know? _____

5. Convert each mixed measurement to a measurement in inches.

a) 3 ft = _36_ in, so

3 ft 5 in = _36_ in + _5_ in

= _41_ in

b) 5 ft = _____ in, so

5 ft 7 in = _____ in + _7_ in

= _____ in

c) 4 ft = _____ in, so

4 ft 2 in = _____ in + _____ in

= _____ in

d) 2 ft = _____ in, so

2 ft 10 in = _____ in + _____ in

= _____ in

e) 6 ft = _____ in, so

6 ft 1 in = _____ in + _____ in

= _____ in

f) 10 ft = _____ in, so

10 ft 11 in = _____ in + _____ in

= _____ in

BONUS ▶

g) 100 ft = _____ in, so

100 ft 10 in = _____ in + _____ in

= _____ in

h) 20 ft = _____ in, so

20 ft 5$\frac{3}{4}$ in = _____ in + _____ in

= _____ in

6. a) Finish a conversion table for feet and inches.

ft	1	2	3					
in	12							

b) For the measurement in inches, write the pair of measurements in feet it is between.

i) _1_ ft < 22 in < (2) ft

ii) _____ ft < 35 in < _____ ft

iii) _____ ft < 47 in < _____ ft

iv) _____ ft < 89 in < _____ ft

c) For each measurement in inches in part b), circle the closest measurement in feet.

d) Write the measurement in inches to the closest foot.

i) 22 inches is about _2_ feet.

ii) 35 inches is about _____ feet.

iii) 47 inches is about _____ feet.

iv) 89 inches is about _____ feet.

BONUS ▶ What is 88$\frac{1}{2}$ inches to the closest foot? _____

MD4-31 Yards

A **yard** (yd) is a unit of measurement for **distance**. Yards are used in the United States.

1 yard

A yardstick is 1 yard long. The yard stick is not drawn to scale.

1. a) Measure the length of your classroom in giant steps. Try to make the giant steps the same length. Length = _____ giant steps

   b) Measure the length of your classroom in yards. Length = _____ yd

   c) Is your giant step longer than a yard or shorter than a yard? _____

   d) Can you use giant steps to estimate distance in yards? _____

2. Estimate the distance. Then measure the actual distance with a yardstick or a measuring tape.

   a) The distance from one end of the chalkboard to the other

   Estimate: about _____ yd   Actual: about _____ yd

   b) The distance from the floor to the door handle

   Estimate: about _____ yd   Actual: about _____ yd

3. Circle the objects that are more than 1 yard long. Cross out the objects that are less than 1 foot long.

1 yard = 3 feet	1 yd = 3 ft

4. Fill in the measurements in feet.

yd	1	2	3	4	5	6	7	8
ft	3							

5. To change a measurement from yards (yd) to feet (ft), what number do you have to multiply by? _____

6. Fill in the missing numbers.

a)

yd	ft
9	
10	
11	

b)

yd	ft
20	
25	
30	

c)

yd	ft
32	
57	
100	

7. Convert the measurement in yards to feet. Then circle the greater measurement.

a) 20 ft   (7 yd)   b) 30 ft   5 yd   c) 19 ft   9 yd

         21 ft

d) 36 ft   10 yd   e) 40 yd   100 ft   f) 100 yd   1,000 ft

8. Write a measurement in feet that is between …

a) 6 yd and 7 yd _____   b) 7 yd and 8 yd _____   c) 12 yd and 13 yd _____

9. Write a measurement in yards that is between …

a) 16 ft and 19 ft _____   b) 28 ft and 32 ft _____   c) 100 ft and 105 ft _____

REMINDER ▶ 1 ft = 12 in. To get a measurement in inches, multiply the measurement in feet by 12.

---

10. a) Make a conversion table from yards to feet, then to inches. Use a calculator.

yd	1	2	3	4	5	6	7	8
ft	*3*							
in	*36*							

b) Use the table to write a measurement in inches between …

i) 3 yd and 4 yd _____   ii) 5 yd and 6 yd _____   iii) 7 yd and 8 yd _____

c) Use the table to write a measurement in yards between …

i) 100 in and 110 in _____   ii) 150 in and 200 in _____   iii) 250 in and 280 in _____

BONUS ▶ What number do you need to multiply by to convert a measurement

     in yards to inches? _____

MD4-32 Inches, Feet, and Yards (Review)

1. Convert all measurements to the smaller unit. Then mark the measurements on the number line.

   a) **L.** 150 ft _____ **A.** 30 yd _____ **B.** 10 yd _____ **D.** 175 ft _____

   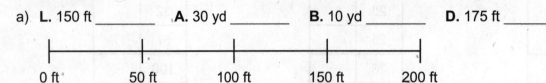

   0 ft   50 ft   100 ft   150 ft   200 ft

   b) **A.** 40 in _____ **E.** 195 in _____ **L.** 13 ft _____ **G.** 9 ft 6 in _____ **E.** 1 ft _____

   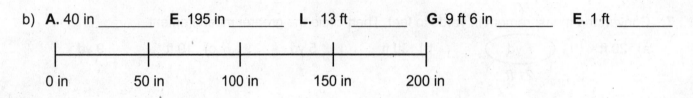

   0 in   50 in   100 in   150 in   200 in

   c) Write the letters from parts a) and b) in order. What symbol of the United States

   do they make? _____ _____ _____ _____   _____ _____ _____ _____

> **REMINDER ▶** Perimeter is the distance around a shape.

2. a) Find the perimeter of each rectangle in yards.
   Hint: Write the lengths of all sides first.

   i)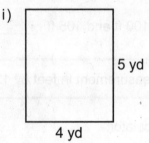
   5 yd
   4 yd

   ii)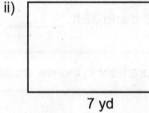
   4 yd
   7 yd

   iii)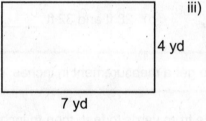
   3 yd
   $2\frac{1}{2}$ yd

   Perimeter = _____ yd   Perimeter = _____ yd   Perimeter = _____ yd

   b) Convert each perimeter from yards to feet.

   i) Perimeter = _____ ft   ii) Perimeter = _____ ft   iii) Perimeter = _____ ft

3. A tiger is 7 feet long. A cobra is 100 inches long. Which is longer, the tiger or the cobra?

4. A snail crawled 30 inches along a branch and 2 feet along a tree trunk.

   a) How much farther did it crawl along the branch than along the tree trunk?

   b) How many inches in total did it crawl? Is the distance more than 1 yard?

5. The pictures show the sizes of a newborn animal and an adult animal.

a) A newborn blue whale is about 24 ft long.
How long is an adult blue whale?

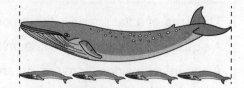

b) A female adult killer whale is about 18 feet long.
How long is a newborn killer whale calf?

c) A newborn polar bear is about 11 inches long.
How long is an adult polar bear?
About how many feet long is an adult polar bear?

6. The Gateway Arch in St. Louis, MO, is 630 ft tall. The Washington Monument in Washington, DC, is 555 ft tall. The White House in Washington, DC, is 70 ft tall.

a) How much taller than the Washington Monument is the Gateway Arch?

b) How many times as tall as the White House is the Gateway Arch?

7. A fence is made of 6 parts. Each part is 4 ft long. How long is the fence?

8. A board is 7 ft long.

a) How many inches long is the board?

b) The board is cut into 3 equal pieces. How long is each piece?

9. a) A window is 3 ft 4 in wide. How wide is the window in inches?

b) To make a nice curtain with folds, the cloth needs to be three times as wide as the window. How wide does the cloth need to be?

BONUS ▶ How wide does the cloth need to be in feet?

MD4-33 Area in Square Centimeters

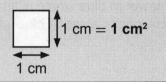

The **area** of a flat shape is the amount of space it takes up.

A **square centimeter** (cm²) is a unit for measuring area.

A square with sides 1 cm has an area of 1 cm².

1 cm = **1 cm²**

1 cm

1. Find the area of the figure in square centimeters.

a)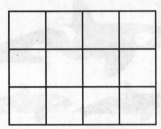

Area = _____ cm²

b)

Area = _____ cm²

c)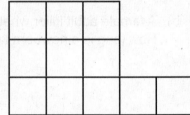

Area = _____ cm²

2. Using a ruler, draw lines to join the marks and divide the rectangle into square centimeters.

a)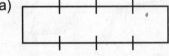

Area = _____ cm²

b)

Area = _____ cm²

c)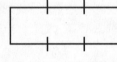

Area = _____ cm²

3. Find the area of the rectangles in square centimeters.

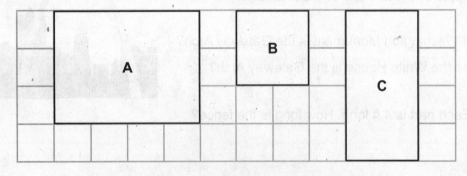

Area of A = _____ cm²   Area of B = _____ cm²   Area of C = _____ cm²

4. Use 1 cm grid paper.

   a) Draw two different rectangles with an area of 8 cm².

   b) Draw two figures that are not rectangles with an area of 8 cm²

   c) Draw several shapes and find their area and perimeter.

   d) Draw a rectangle with an area of 8 cm² and perimeter of 12 cm.

MD4-34 Area of Rectangles

1. Write a multiplication statement for the array.

a)

b)

c)

d)

_____   _____   _____   _____

2. Draw a dot in each box. Then write a multiplication statement that tells you the number of boxes in the rectangle.

a)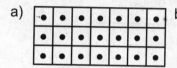

b)

c)

d)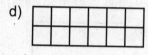

_____ $3 \times 7 = 21$ _____   _____   _____   _____

3. Write the number of boxes along the width and the length of the rectangle.
Then write a multiplication equation for the area of the rectangle (in square units).

a) 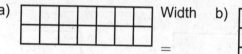 Width

= _____

Length = _____

_____

b) Width

= _____

Length = _____

_____

c) 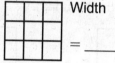 Width

= _____

Length = _____

_____

4. Using a ruler, draw lines to join the marks and divide the rectangle into square centimeters.
Write a multiplication equation for the area of the rectangle in square centimeters.

a)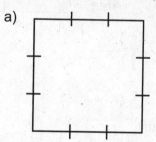

Area = _____

b)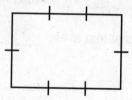

Area = _____

c)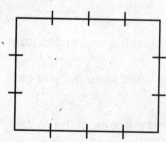

Area = _____

5. How can you find the area of a rectangle from its length and width?

_____

_____

6. Measure the length and width of the rectangle. Find the area. Include the units!

a)

b)

c)

_____   _____   _____

7. Area is also measured in other square units. Predict the names of the units below.

a)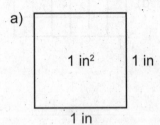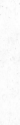

1 in²   1 in

1 in

_____*square inch*_____

b)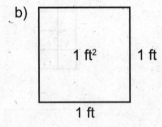

1 ft²   1 ft

1 ft

_____

c)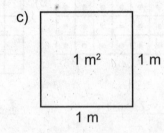

1 m²   1 m

1 m

_____

8. a) Calculate the area of the rectangle (include the units).

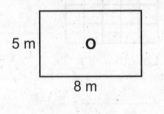
5 m   **O**
8 m

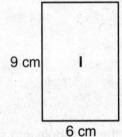
9 cm   **I**
6 cm

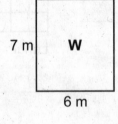
7 m   **W**
6 m

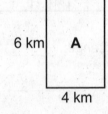
6 km   **A**
4 km

Area = _____   Area = _____   Area = _____   Area = _____

b) List the rectangles from least area to greatest area: _____ , _____ , _____ , _____

What state did you get? _____

9. Find the area of the rectangle using the length and the width. Include the units!

a) Width = 5 m   Length = 7 m   b) Width = 2 m   Length = 9 m   c) Width = 6 cm   Length = 8 cm

Area = ___*35 m²*___   Area = _____   Area = _____

d) Width = 11 in   Length = 7 in   e) Width = 12 ft   Length = 9 ft   f) Width = 3 yd   Length = 12 yd

Area = _____   Area = _____   Area = _____

MD4-35 Problems with Area and Perimeter of Rectangles

> Area of rectangle = width × length

1. Find the area of the rectangle.

   a) Width = 3 m   Length = 6 m

   Area = _____ × _____

   = _____

   b) Width = 2 m   Length = 9 m

   Area = _____ × _____

   = _____

   c) Width = 6 cm   Length = 8 cm

   Area = _____ × _____

   = _____

2. Write an equation for the area of the rectangle. Then find the unknown width.

   a) Width = w m

   Length = 5 m

   Area = 15 m²

   $w \times 5 = 15$

   $w = 15 \div 5$

   $= 3$

   b) Width = w m

   Length = 2 m

   Area = 12 m²

   _____

   _____

   _____

   c) Width = w cm

   Length = 6 cm

   Area = 24 cm²

   _____

   _____

   _____

3. Write an equation for the area of the rectangle. Then find the unknown length.

   a) Width = 5 m

   Length = l m

   Area = 20 m²

   $5 \times l = 20$

   $l = 20 \div 5$

   $= 4$

   b) Width = 7 m

   Length = l m

   Area = 21 m²

   _____

   _____

   _____

   c) Width = 10 in

   Length = l in

   Area = 40 in²

   _____

   _____

   _____

4. a) A rectangle has an area of 24 ft² and a width of 3 ft. What is its length?

   b) A rectangle has an area of 10 cm² and a length of 5 cm. What is its width?

   c) A square has an area of 9 cm². What is its width?

5. A rectangle with width 3 cm and length 4 cm has area 12 cm².

   a) Find a different pair of numbers that multiply to equal 12.

   b) Draw a rectangle with width and length equal to your numbers.

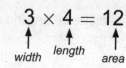

6. a) Measure the length and the width of each rectangle in centimeters. Find the perimeter and area of each rectangle. Write the answers in the table.

A
5 cm

3 cm

B

C

D

E

F

Shape	Perimeter	Area
A	3 cm + 5 cm + 3 cm + 5 cm = 16 cm	3 cm × 5 cm = 15 cm²
B		
C		
D		
E		
F		

b) Shape E has a greater perimeter than shape A. Does it also have a greater area? _____

c) Name two rectangles that have the same perimeter and different areas. _____ and _____

d) Write the shapes in order from greatest perimeter to least perimeter. _____

e) Write the shapes in order from greatest area to least area. _____

f) Are the orders in parts d) and e) the same? _____

g) Describe the difference between *perimeter* and *area*.

7. Will you use area or perimeter to find ...

a) the amount of paper needed to cover a bulletin board? _____

b) the distance around a field? _____

c) the amount of carpet needed for a room? _____

d) the amount of ribbon needed to make a border for a picture? _____

MD4-36 Area (Advanced)

1. **a)** Calculate the area of each figure.

i) A B C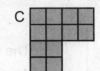

ii) A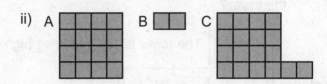

Area of A = _____

Area of B = _____

Area of C = _____

Area of A = _____

Area of B = _____

Area of C = _____

iii) A C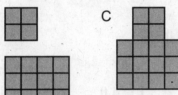

B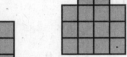

iv) A 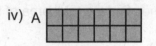 C

B

Area of A = _____

Area of B = _____

Area of C = _____

Area of A = _____

Area of B = _____

Area of C = _____

b) Draw a line to show how shape C can be divided into rectangles A and B in part a).

c) How can you get the area of shape C from the areas of rectangles A and B? Write an equation.

Area of C = _____

2. Draw a line to divide the figure into two rectangles. Use the areas of the rectangles to find the total area of the figure.

a)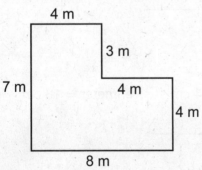

4 m
3 m
7 m
4 m
4 m
8 m

b)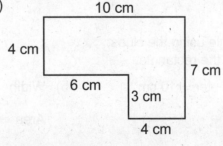

10 cm
4 cm
6 cm
7 cm
3 cm
4 cm

c)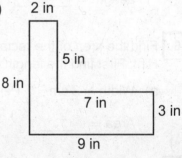

2 in
5 in
8 in
7 in
3 in
9 in

Area of rectangle 1 = _____

Area of rectangle 2 = _____

Total area = _____

Area of rectangle 1 = _____

Area of rectangle 2 = _____

Total area = _____

Area of rectangle 1 = _____

Area of rectangle 2 = _____

Total area = _____

3. a) A building is 8 stories high. The wing is 5 stories high. How many stories high is the tower?

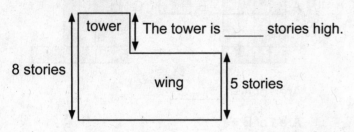

The tower is _____ stories high.

b) The tower of a building is 10 m wide. The base is 50 m wide. How wide is the wing?

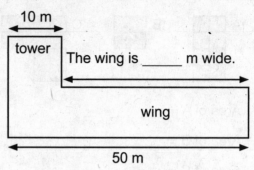

The wing is _____ m wide.

4. Find the missing side lengths. Divide the figure into two rectangles and find their areas. Then find the total area of the figure.

a)

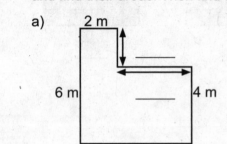

b)

Area of rectangle 1 = _____

Area of rectangle 2 = _____

Total area = _____

Area of rectangle 1 = _____

Area of rectangle 2 = _____

Total area = _____

5. Find the length of the rectangle.

a) Width = 2 cm   Perimeter = 12 cm

Length = _____

b) Width = 4 cm   Perimeter = 14 cm

Length = _____

6. Find the area of the rectangle using the clues.
Hint: First find the length of the rectangle.

a) Width = 2 cm   Perimeter = 10 cm

Area = _____

b) Width = 4 cm   Perimeter = 18 cm

Area = _____

7. On grid paper, draw a **square** with the given perimeter. Then find the area of the square.

a) Perimeter = 12 cm   Area = _____

b) Perimeter = 20 cm   Area = _____

MD4-37 Problems and Puzzles

1. On grid paper, draw a rectangle with …

  a) an area of 10 square units and a perimeter of 14 units.

  b) an area of 12 square units and a perimeter of 14 units.

2. a) Find the area of the shaded word.

  b) There are 33 squares in the grid.
      How can you use your answer to part a)
      to find the number of unshaded squares?

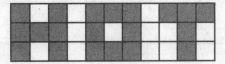

3. Raj wants to build a rectangular flowerbed of width 2 ft and perimeter 12 ft.

  a) Sketch the flowerbed on the grid.

  b) What is the length of the flowerbed?

  c) Raj wants to build a fence around the flowerbed.
      Fencing costs $3 per foot. How much will the fencing cost?

  d) Raj will plant 2 sunflower seeds on each square foot
      of land. Each sunflower seed costs 2¢.
      How much will the flowers cost altogether?

Note: The side of each square
in the grid represents 1 foot.

4. a) Draw two rectangles to show that figures with the same area
      can have different perimeters.

  b) Draw two rectangles to show that figures with the same perimeter
      can have different areas.

5. The area of your thumbnail is about 1 square centimeter (1 cm²).
Estimate the area of this rectangle using your thumbnail.
Then measure the sides of the rectangle and find its actual area.

6. On grid paper, draw a figure made of four squares.
Each square must share at least one edge with another square.

  a) How many different figures can you create?

  b) What is the area of the figures?

  c) Which figure has the smallest perimeter?

  d) Ella thinks that two figures with the same perimeter and the same area
      have to be exactly the same shape and size. Is she correct? Explain.

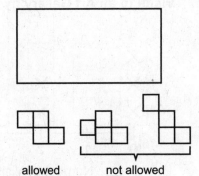

allowed   not allowed

MD4-38 Line Plots (Review)

All line plots have a number line, a title, and a label.

Number of Books Ms. K's Class Read This Week ◄——— title

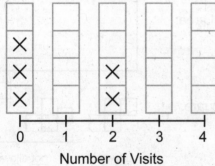

1   2   3   4   5   6   ◄——— number line

Number of Books   ◄——— label

1. Answer the questions about the line plot shown above.

   a) How many people read 4 books? _____

   b) How many people read 3 books? _____

   c) How many more people read 3 books than 4 books? _____

   d) What is the most common number of books read? _____

2. Put the data values on the line plot. Cross out each value as you use it.
   The first one has been started for you.

   a) 3̸   3̸   3̸   4̸   4̸   b) 2   3   3   5   6   3

      3   3   3   3   4   4   3   2   6   5   6

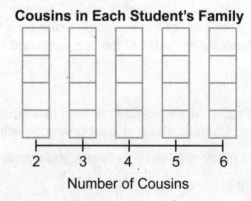

Visits to an Art Gallery by Each Student

0   1   2   3   4

Number of Visits

Cousins in Each Student's Family

2   3   4   5   6

Number of Cousins

3. Fill in the blanks to check your work in Question 2. Are your answers the same?
   If not, find your mistake.

   Number of data values in a) _____   Number of Xs on finished line plot _____

   Number of data values in b) _____   Number of Xs on finished line plot _____

4. Here are the names of students in a Fourth Grade class.

Adam	Dinesh	Fadi
Freya	George	Jade
Jacqueline	Maurizio	Musa
Xavier	Yuna	Zoe

a) The shortest name is _____. It has _____ letters.

  Put this as the lowest number on the number line below.

b) Finish writing the numbers on the number line.

c) Count the letters in each name to build a line plot.

  Cross out the names as you use them.

d) Add a title and label to finish the line plot.

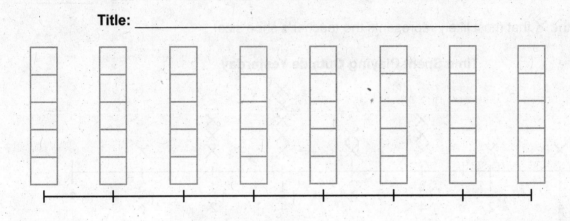

Title: _____

Label: _____

5. Use your line plot from Question 4 to answer these questions.

a) How long is the longest name in the class? _____ letters long

b) How many people have at least six letters in their name? _____

c) What is the most common number of letters in a name? _____

d) Is there a name in the class with 0 letters? _____

e) Can there be a name in *any* class with 0 letters? _____

f) How many letters longer than the shortest name is the longest name? _____

MD4-39 Fractions on Line Plots

Shoe Sizes in Our Class

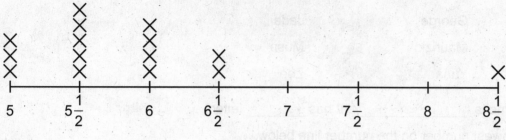

Shoe Size

1. a) How many people wear shoe size 6? _____

    b) What is the most common shoe size? _____

    c) What is the difference between the largest shoe size and the smallest shoe size? _____

    d) Circle the X that most likely represents the teacher's shoe size.

Time Spent Playing Outside Yesterday

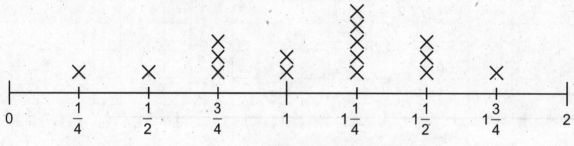

Time (hours)

2. a) How many people spent $\frac{3}{4}$ of an hour playing outside? _____

    b) Of all the children, Yeeling spent the most time playing outside.

    How much time did she spend playing outside? _____ hours

    BONUS ▶ Yeeling started playing outside at 1:30 p.m.
    What time did she come inside? _____

    c) Of all the children, Ravi spent the least time playing outside.

    How much time did he spend playing outside? _____ hours

    BONUS ▶ Ravi started playing outside at 11:50 a.m.
    What time did he come inside? _____

    d) How much more time did Yeeling spend playing outside than Ravi? _____ hours more

    e) How many people played outside for less than an hour? _____

3. **a)** Measure the heights of the flowers to the nearest eighth of an inch.

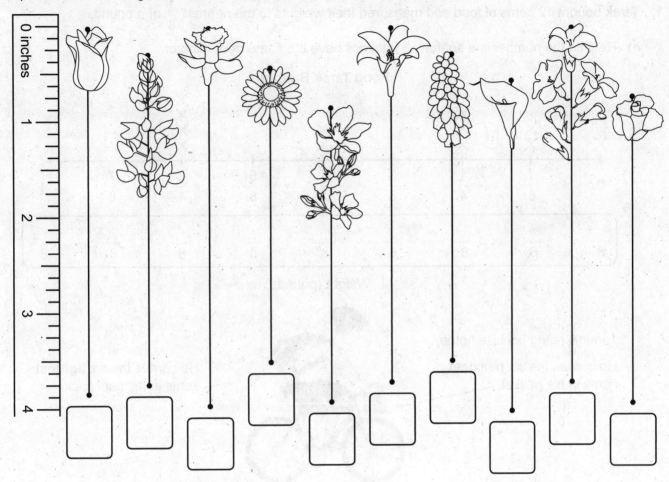

b) Draw a line plot to show the data.

Title: _____

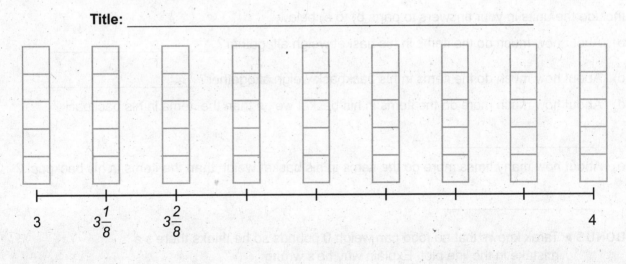

Label: _____

c) How much taller than the shortest flower is the tallest flower? _____

MD4-40 Line Plots (Advanced)

1. Tarek bought 12 items of food and measured their weights to the nearest $\frac{1}{8}$ of a pound.

   a) Rewrite the number line so that all fractions have the same denominator.

Food Tarek Bought

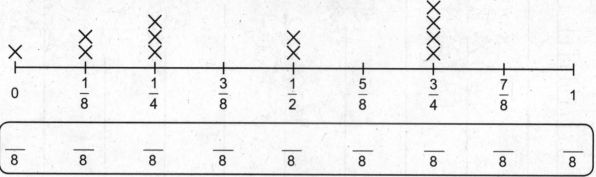

Weight (pounds)

Tarek is riding his bike home.

He carries the six **heaviest** items in his basket.

He carries the six **lightest** items in his backpack.

Include the units in your answers to parts b) to e) below.

b) About how much do the items in his basket weigh altogether? _____

c) About how much do the items in his backpack weigh altogether? _____

d) About how much more do the items in his basket weigh than the items in his backpack?

   _____

e) About how many times more do the items in his basket weigh than the items in his backpack?

   _____

BONUS ▶ Tarek knows that no food can weigh 0 pounds so he thinks there's a mistake in the line plot. Explain why he's wrong.

_____

_____

G4-14 Lines, Line Segments, and Rays

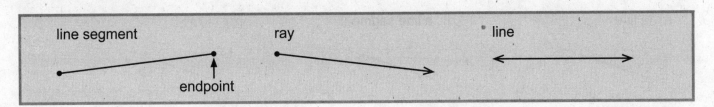

line segment   ray   line

endpoint

1. How many endpoints does each object have?

   a) line segment _____   b) ray _____   c) line _____

2. Identify each picture as a line, line segment, or ray.

   a)

   _____

   b)

   _____

   c)

   _____

   d)

   _____

   e)

   _____

   f)

   _____

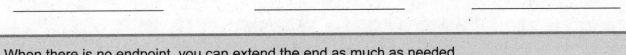

When there is no endpoint, you can extend the end as much as needed.

endpoint

this end can
be extended

3. Extend the line at both ends. Name the point or points that are on the line.

   a) •A

   •B

   _____

   b) •A

   •B

   •C

   _____

   c) •A

   •B

   •C

   _____

4. Extend the ray at one end.

   a)

   b)

   c)

5. Draw arrows or dots to make ...

a) a line

b) a line segment

c) a ray

Which part has two answers? _____

6. Sketch ...

a) a line

b) a ray

c) a line segment

7. Use a ruler to draw ...

a) a ray and a point on it

b) a ray and a point not on the ray

8. Extend the lines and the rays.

a)

b)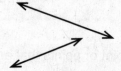

c)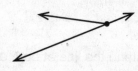

9. Extend each ray where possible. Name the points that are on the ray.

a)

_____

b)

_____

c)

_____

10. a) Draw a line segment and a point on it.

b) Draw a line and a point not on the line.

Geometry 4-14

A point where lines, rays, or line segments meet is called an **intersection point**.

intersection point

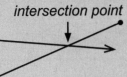

11. Circle the intersection points.

a)
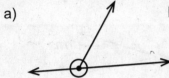

b)

c)
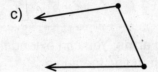

d)

12. Draw ...

    a) two intersecting line segments

    b) two intersecting rays

    c) a line intersecting a ray

    d) three lines intersecting at the same point

13. Do the lines, rays, or line segments intersect? Extend them where possible to check.

a)
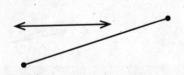

_____

b)
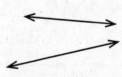

_____

c)
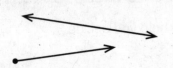

_____

d)
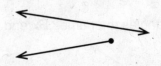

_____

G4-15 Angles

An **angle** is the space between two rays with the same endpoint. When two rays have the same endpoint, we do not have to draw a dot to show the endpoint.

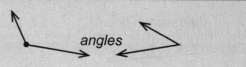

angles

1. Circle the pictures that show angles.

An angle has a **vertex** and **arms**. You can extend the arms as much as needed without changing the angle.

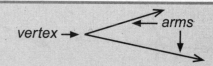

2. Circle the vertex and extend the arms of each angle.

 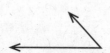 

The **size** of an angle is the amount of rotation between the arms.

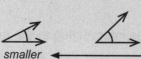

smaller ← → larger

3. Circle the larger angle.

a)

b)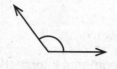

c)

d)

These angles are the same size, even though one looks larger. The amount of rotation between the arms (how much you turn one arm to get the other) is the same in both angles.

 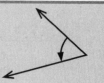

4. Are the angles the same? Extend the arms that look shorter to help you decide.

a)   _____

b)  _____

5. Circle the larger angle. Then extend the arms that look shorter to check your answer.

a) 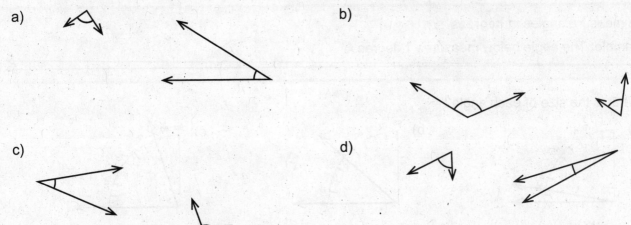   b)

c)   d)

REMINDER ▶ Angles equal to the corners of a square are called right angles. You can use a corner of a sheet of paper to compare an angle with a right angle.

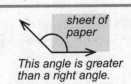

sheet of paper

This angle is greater than a right angle.

---

6. Compare each angle to a right angle using the corner of a sheet of paper. Mark each angle as *less* than a right angle or *greater* than a right angle.

a) 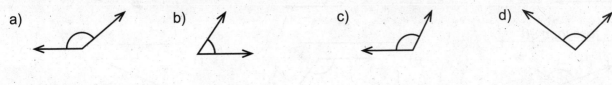   b)   c)   d)

_____   _____   _____   _____

Angles that are less than a right angle are called **acute angles**. Angles that are greater than a right angle are called **obtuse angles**.

acute angle   *obtuse angle*

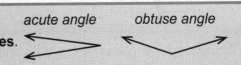

---

7. Identify each angle as *acute* or *obtuse*.

a)    b)    c)    d)

_____   _____   _____   _____

e) 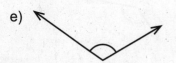   f)   g)   h)

_____   _____   _____   _____

---

 8. a) Draw an acute angle.   b) Draw an obtuse angle.

G4-16 Measuring Angles

We measure angles in **degrees**.

Example: The angle below measures 1 degree.

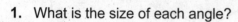

1. What is the size of each angle?

   a)

   10 degrees

   b)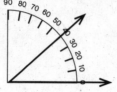

   _____

   c)

   _____

We use a small raised circle after the number instead of the word degree: 1 degree = 1°.
A right angle measures 90°.

2. Identify each angle as less than 90° or more than 90°.

   a)

   less than 90°

   b)

   _____

   c)

   _____

   d)

   _____

   e)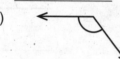

   _____

   f)

   _____

Acute angles are less than a right angle. They measure between 0° and 90°.
Obtuse angles are greater than a right angle. They measure between 90° and 180°.

3. Identify each angle as *acute* or *obtuse*.

   a)

   _____

   b)

   _____

   c)

   _____

   d)

   _____

   e)

   _____

   f)

   _____

4. Identify each angle measure as that of an *acute* or an *obtuse* angle.

   a) 45° _____

   b) 120° _____

   c) 76° _____

   d) 92° _____

   e) 175° _____

   f) 15° _____

To measure an angle, we use a **protractor**.

A protractor has 180 subdivisions of 1° around its curved side.
It has two scales, to measure angles starting from either side.

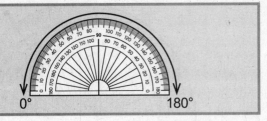

0°   180°

5. Identify the angle as acute or obtuse.
    Circle the two numbers that the arm of the angle passes through.
    Pick the correct angle measure. (Example: if you said the angle is acute,
    pick the number that is less than 90.)

a)

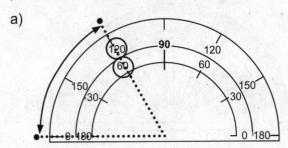

The angle is _____ *acute* _____ .

The angle measures ___ *60°* ___ .

b)

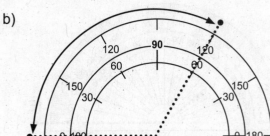

The angle is _____ .

The angle measures _____ .

c)

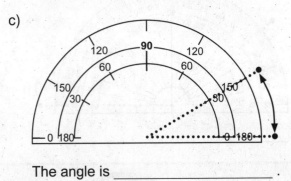

The angle is _____ .

The angle measures _____ .

d)

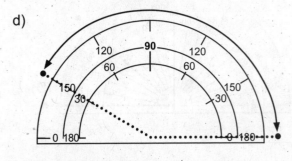

The angle is _____ .

The angle measures _____ .

6. Identify the angle as acute or obtuse. Then write the measure of the angle.

a)

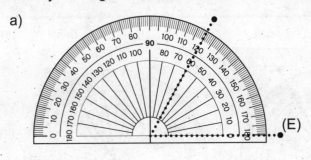

(E)

b)

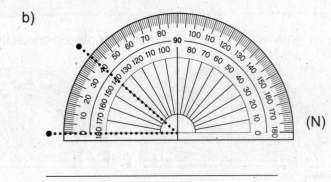

(N)

_____

_____

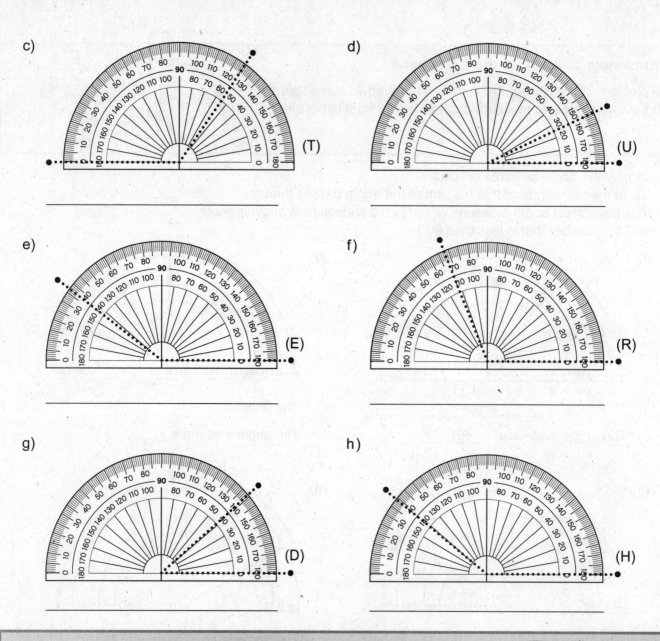

c) _____ (T)

d) _____ (U)

e) _____ (E)

f) _____ (R)

g) _____ (D)

h) _____ (H)

Each protractor has a **base line** and an **origin**.

To measure an angle, line up one arm of the angle with the base line.
Place the vertex of the angle at the origin of the protractor.

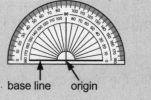

base line   origin

7. a) In which picture is the protractor placed correctly? _____

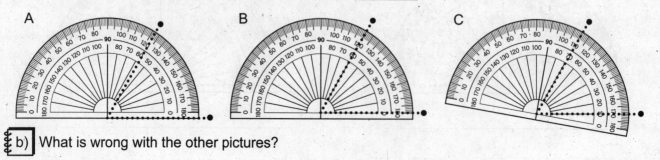

A   B   C

b) What is wrong with the other pictures?

8. Measure the angle using a protractor, and write your answer in the box.
Hint: Use a ruler to extend the arms in parts e) and f).

a)
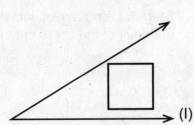 (I)

b)
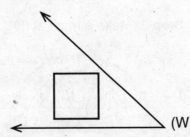 (W)

c)
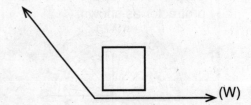 (W)

d)
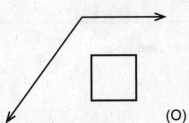 (O)

e)
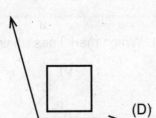 (D)

f)
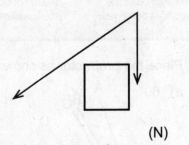 (N)

9. Measure the marked angle using a protractor. Write your answer in the blank.

a)

_____

b)

_____

c)

_____

10. a) Draw …

i) a right angle

ii) an acute angle

iii) an obtuse angle

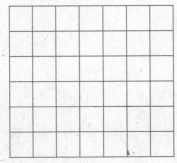

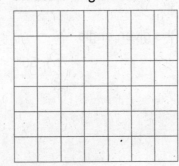

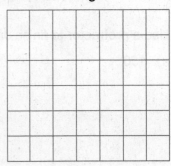

b) Measure each of your angles.

i) _____

ii) _____

iii) _____

11. Draw five angles and use a protractor to measure them.

G4-17 Drawing Angles

To draw a 60° angle:

Step 1: Draw a ray. Place the protractor as shown.

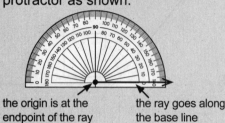

the origin is at the endpoint of the ray

the ray goes along the base line

Step 2: Make a mark at 60°.

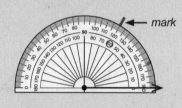

← mark

Step 3: Using a ruler, join the endpoint of the ray to the mark.

← mark

1. Place the protractor as shown in Step 1. Which mark lines up with the given angle?

a) 60°

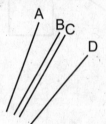

b) 140°

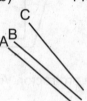

2. Finish drawing the angle.

a) 70°

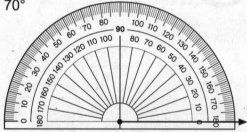

b) 125°

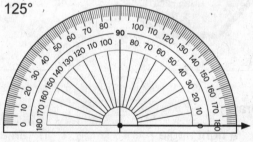

3. Use a protractor to finish drawing the given angle.

a) 150°

b) 55°

4. Use a protractor to construct the angle.

a) 45°   b) 80°   c) 50°   d) 145°   e) 62°   f) 128°

G4-18 Adding Angles

We can use letters to represent angles.

1. Measure the angles.

a)
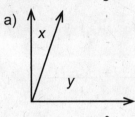

x = _____ °   y = _____ °

b)
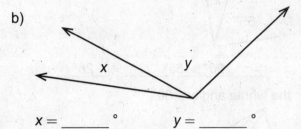

x = _____ °   y = _____ °

2. a) Measure the small angles and the whole angle.

i)
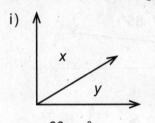

x = __60__ °   y = __30__ °

whole angle = __90__ °

ii)
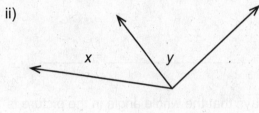

x = _____ °   y = _____ °

whole angle = _____ °

iii)
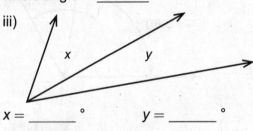

x = _____ °   y = _____ °

whole angle = _____ °

iv)
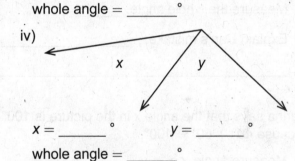

x = _____ °   y = _____ °

whole angle = _____ °

b) How can you get the measure of the whole angle from the measure of the small angles? _____

3. Find the measure of the whole angle by adding the measures of the small angles.

a)
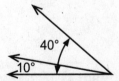

the whole angle = ____ + ____ = ____

b)
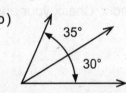

the whole angle = ____ + ____ = ____

c)
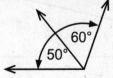

the whole angle = ____ + ____ = ____

d)
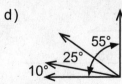

the whole angle = ____ + ____ + ____ = ____

4. Find *x*.

a) the whole angle = 90°

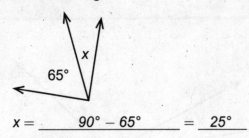

$x =$ ___90° − 65°___ = ___25°___

b) the whole angle = 120°

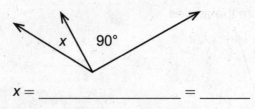

$x =$ _____ = _____

c) the whole angle = 80°

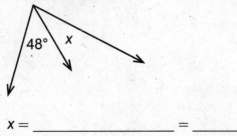

$x =$ _____ = _____

d) the whole angle = 150°

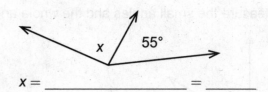

$x =$ _____ = _____

5. Dan says that the whole angle in the picture is 140°,
because 80° + 60° = 140°.

a) Measure the whole angle. _____

b) Explain Dan's mistake. _____

_____

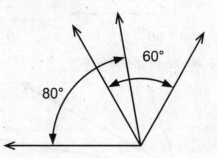

6. Marina says that the angle *x* in the picture is 100°,
because 40° + 60° = 100°.

a) Measure angle *x*. $x =$ _____

b) Explain Marina's mistake. _____

_____

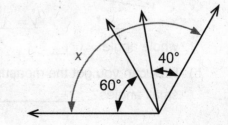

7. The whole angle is 160°. Find *x*. Check your answer by measuring.

a)

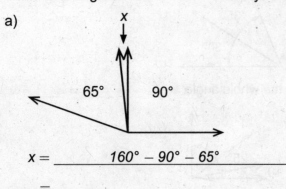

$x =$ ___160° − 90° − 65°___

= _____

b)

$x =$ _____

= _____

G4-19 Adding Angles (Advanced)

The whole angle is 80°. Ben wants to find the measure of angle *x*.
He writes and solves an equation:

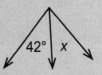

$x + 42° = 80°$

$x = 80° - 42°$

$\quad = 38°$

1. a) Write an equation to find *x*.

    i)   the whole angle is 90°

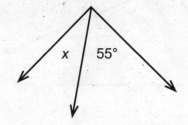

    ii)   the whole angle is 150°

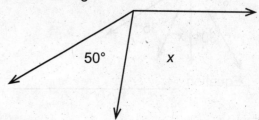

    iii)   the whole angle is 103°

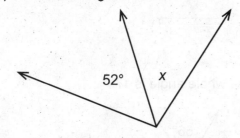

    iv)   the whole angle is 123°

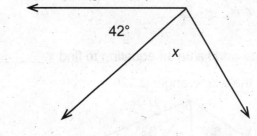

  b)   Solve your equations from part a) to find *x*. Do parts iii) and iv) in your notebook.

    i) $x + 55° = 90°$

           $x = 90° - 55°$

           $x = 35°$

    ii)

  c)   Measure angle *x* to check your answers in part b).

2. Write and solve an equation to find *x*.

  a)   the whole angle is 110°

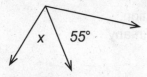

  b)   the whole angle is 70°

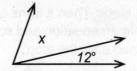

The whole angle is 150°. Ben wants to find the measure of angle x. He writes and solves an equation:

$45° + x + 35° = 150°$
$x + 80° = 150°$
$x = 150° - 80°$
$= 70°$

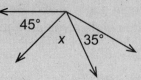

3. Write and solve an equation to find x. Then measure angle x to check your answer.

a) the whole angle is 90°

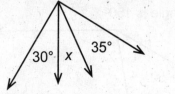

Equation: _____

$x =$ _____ °

b) the whole angle is 160°

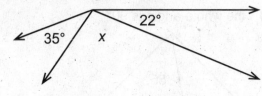

Equation: _____

$x =$ _____ °

4. Write and solve an equation to find x.

a) the whole angle is 126°

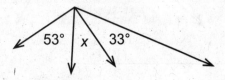

Equation: _____

$x =$ _____ °

b) the whole angle is 173°

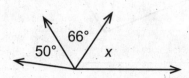

Equation: _____

$x =$ _____ °

c) the whole angle is 121°

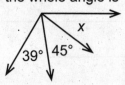

Equation: _____

$x =$ _____ °

BONUS ▶

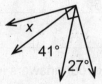

Equation: _____

$x =$ _____ °

5. A sprinkler turns 25° and stops. Then it turns some more in the same direction. It turns a total of 60°. Write an equation and solve the equation to find how many degrees the sprinkler turned after the stop.

G4-20 Angles as Fractions of a Circle

1. a) How many quarter turns are in a full turn? _____

   b) What angle does a quarter turn make? _____

   c) Mark the right angles on the picture at right.

   d) How many degrees are in a full turn? _____ × _____ = _____

   There are _____ in a full turn.

2. A minute hand turns 1° in 10 seconds.

   a) How many seconds does it take the minute hand to rotate 6°? _____

   b) How many seconds does it take the minute hand to rotate 30°? _____

   How many minutes is that? _____

   c) How many seconds does it take the minute hand to rotate 360°? _____

   How many minutes is that? _____

   d) What fraction of a full circle does a minute hand turn in 1 hour? _____

   Does your answer in part c) make sense? _____ Explain. _____

   _____

3. A sprinkler turns 1° every second. It turns a total of 57°.

   How many 1° turns has the sprinkler made? _____

4. a) A sprinkler turns 28°, stops, and then turns another 15° in the same direction.

   How many degrees did the sprinkler turn altogether? _____

   b) A sprinkler turns 150°, stops, and then turns 73° in the opposite direction.

   How many more degrees should the sprinkler turn to get back to the starting position? _____

REMINDER ▶ $\frac{1}{3}$ of 360 = 360 ÷ 3 = 120

$\frac{2}{3}$ is 2 × $\frac{1}{3}$, so $\frac{2}{3}$ of 360 = 2 × 120 = 240

---

5. Find the fraction of 360.

   a) $\frac{1}{10}$ of 360 = _____ = _____

   $\frac{3}{10}$ of 360 = _____ = _____

   b) $\frac{1}{5}$ of 360 = _____ = _____

   $\frac{2}{5}$ of 360 = _____ = _____

The shaded part is $\frac{1}{6}$ of the circle.

There are 360° in a full turn.

The angle in the shaded part is 360° ÷ 6 = 60°.

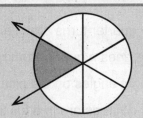

6. Use a protractor to check that the shaded angle in the box above is 60°.

7. Fill in the blanks. Use a protractor to check the angles.

a)

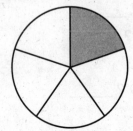

What fraction of the circle is shaded? _____

What is the angle? $\dfrac{\boxed{}}{\boxed{}}$ of 360° = _____

b)

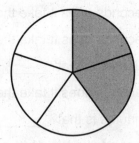

What fraction of the circle is shaded? _____

What is the angle? $\dfrac{\boxed{}}{\boxed{}}$ of 360° = _____

c)

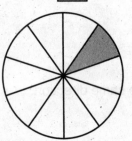

What fraction of the circle is shaded? _____

What is the angle? $\dfrac{\boxed{}}{\boxed{}}$ of 360° = _____

d)

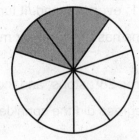

What fraction of the circle is shaded? _____

What is the angle? $\dfrac{\boxed{}}{\boxed{}}$ of 360° = _____

e)

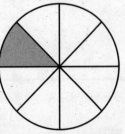

What fraction of the circle is shaded? _____

What is the angle? $\dfrac{\boxed{}}{\boxed{}}$ of 360° = _____

f)

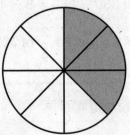

What fraction of the circle is shaded? _____

What is the angle? $\dfrac{\boxed{}}{\boxed{}}$ of 360° = _____

G4-21 Angles in Shapes

1. Mark each right angle in the shape with a small square, each acute angle with an *A*,
   and each obtuse angle with an *O*.

   a)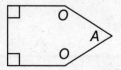

   b)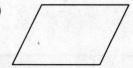

   c)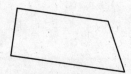

   d)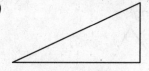

   e)

   f)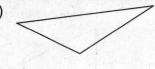

2. Measure the angles in each triangle.

   a)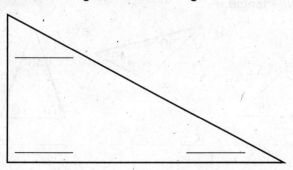

   b)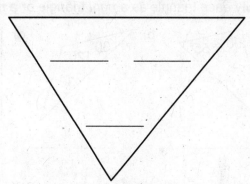

3. Extend the arms of the angle marked with an arc. Then measure the angle.

   a)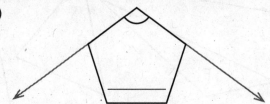

   b)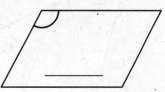

   c)

   d)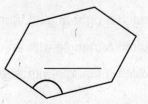

4. Measure all the angles in the triangle. Extend the arms of the angles if needed.

a)

b)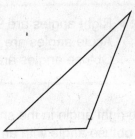

Triangles that have a right angle (90°) are called **right-angled** triangles or **right triangles** for short.

right triangles   *not right triangles*

5. Classify each triangle as a *right* triangle or a *not right* triangle.

a)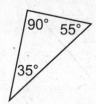
90° 55° 35°

b)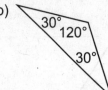
30° 120° 30°

c)
45° 90° 45°

d)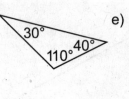
30° 110° 40°

e)
40° 70° 70°

_____   _____   _____

6. a) Mark the right angles in the triangles. Check with a corner of a sheet of paper.

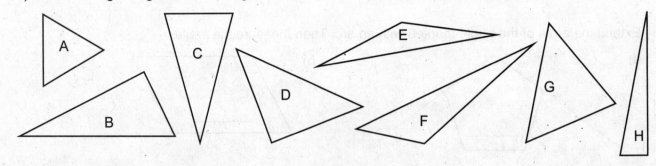

A B C D E F G H

b) Which triangles are right triangles? _____

7. Do not use a ruler or a protractor.

a) Sketch a right-angled triangle.

b) Sketch a triangle with an obtuse angle.

c) Sketch a triangle with three acute angles.

G4-22 Classifying Shapes

REMINDER ▶

Perpendicular lines make a right angle.

Parallel lines never meet, even if extended. They are always the same distance apart.

1. a) Mark right angles with squares. Mark parallel sides with arrows.

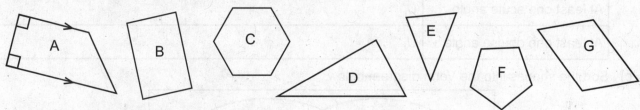

b) Sort the shapes into the table below.

At least one pair of parallel sides	A,
At least one pair of perpendicular sides	A,

c) Sort the shapes into the Venn diagram below.

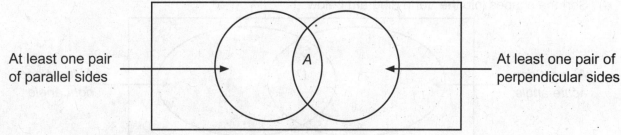

At least one pair of parallel sides → [A] ← At least one pair of perpendicular sides

d) A **right triangle** is a triangle that has a right angle.
Sketch a right triangle and label it H.
Sketch a triangle that is not a right triangle. Label it J.

e) Add H and J to the table in part b) and to the Venn diagram in part c).

BONUS ▶

f) In which part of the Venn diagram would a square go? _____

g) Can there be a triangle that goes into the central area of the Venn diagram? Explain.

REMINDER ▶ Right angles are 90°.
Acute angles are more than 0° and less than 90°.
Obtuse angles are more than 90° and less than 180°.

---

2. a) Mark acute angles with an A and obtuse angles with an O.

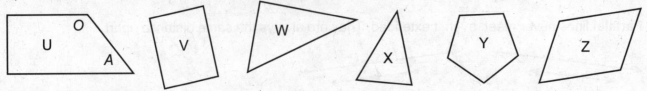

b) Sort the shapes into the table below.

At least one acute angle	U,
At least one obtuse angle	U,

c) Sort the shapes into the Venn diagram below.

At least one acute angle

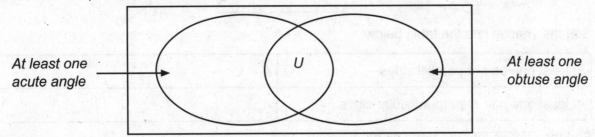

At least one obtuse angle

d) Sort the shapes into the Venn diagram below.

At least one acute angle

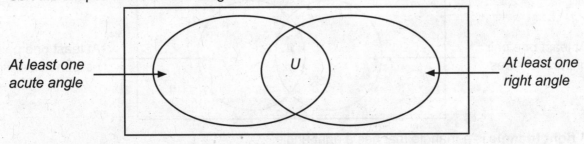

At least one right angle

e) Draw three different right triangles. Label them R, S, and T.

f) Add R, S, and T to the Venn diagram in part d).

Did they go into the same part of the diagram? _____

g) Can there be a right triangle that does not go into the same area of the

Venn diagram as R, S, and T? _____

3. **a)** Draw three angles that measure 45° using the given rays as arms.

b) Circle all the angles that might measure 45° in these shapes.

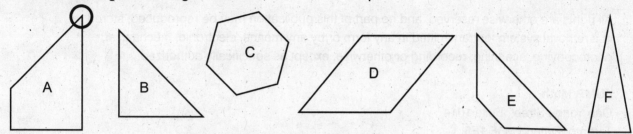

c) Measure the angles. Put a check mark next to the angles that actually measure 45°.

d) Which shapes have a 45° angle? _____

4. **a)** Draw three angles that measure 135°, pointing in different directions.

b) Circle all the angles that might measure 135° in these shapes.

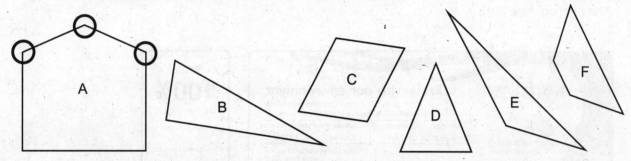

c) Measure the angles. Put a check mark next to the angles that actually measure 135°.

d) Which shapes have a 135° angle? _____

e) Draw three angles that measure 70°. Have the angles point in different directions.

f) Measure the angles in part b) that might be 70°. Then sort the shapes into the table.

Two angles of 70°	
One angle of 70°	
No angles of 70°	

JUMP Math
One Yonge Street, Suite 1014
Toronto, Ontario M5E 1E5
Canada
www.jumpmath.org

Writers: Dr. John Mighton, Dr. Sindi Sabourin, Dr. Anna Klebanov, Dr. Sohrab Rahbar, Julie Lorinc
Editors: Dimitra Chronopoulos, Debbie Davies-Wright, Ewa Krynski
Layout and Illustrations: Linh Lam, Gabriella Kerr
Cover Design: Blakeley Words+Pictures
Cover Photograph: © LuckyOliver.com

ISBN 978-1-927457-13-9

First printing June 2013

Preserving our environment

Jump Math chose to print the pages of this book on recycled paper and saved these resources[1]:

energy	water	greenhouse gases	solid waste
37 million BTUs	149,417 L	3,302 kg	1,199 kg

Printed by **Webcom Inc.** on Legacy Brite 100%

RECYCLED
100%
RECYCLABLE
Legacy Brite 100%

Printed by **Webcom Inc.**

ANCIENT FOREST™ FRIENDLY

84 trees were saved for our forests

[1]Estimates were made using the Environmental Defense Paper Calculator.

This book was manufactured without the use of additional coatings or processes, and was assembled using the latest equipment to achieve almost zero waste. Manufacturing this book in Canada ensures compliance with strict environmental practices and eliminates the need for international freight, which is a major contributor to global air pollution.

Printed and bound in Canada